Performance Test: Three Step System, Volume 1

Performance Test: Three Step System, Volume 1

9 Official PTs: 2024, 2023, 2022, 2021, and Oct 2020

Ray Hayden, JD

This book is published by VDO1.

ISBN-13 (Paperback): 978-1-970586-02-2

Disclaimer

This publication is a study guide intended for educational purposes only and is not a substitute for legal advice, instruction, or training. While the author has authorization to use the official **California General Bar Exam (CGBX)** materials as a basis for the content (we all do), the author and publisher make no representations or warranties concerning the accuracy, completeness, or suitability of the information herein. The law changes rapidly, and readers are advised to consult the most current statutory and case law. **The author and publisher specifically disclaim any liability for loss or risk, personal or otherwise, which is incurred as a consequence, directly or indirectly, of the use and application of any of the contents of this study guide.**

Dedication

This volume is **dedicated to all law students**, to those who have since entered the legal profession, and to **all who continue to fight the good fight for the opportunity to serve.**

I extend my deep appreciation to my wife, Lisa, whose dedication, patience, advice, and suggestions were invaluable throughout this project.

Thanks to a fellow author, Tanja, from Germany. Her experiences with publishing have been insightful and very helpful. Of note, I do not speak German, but she understands enough English, and we can communicate regardless!

To some of the folks who have inspired me with their efforts and success. In no particular order: Perry, Gil, Jules, Benjamin, Max, Windie, Maya, Estela, Lizalou, Ashley, Shirleen, Crystal, Dmitry, Liberty, Cynthia, Victoria, and so many more who continue to fight the good fight for evolution of the Admission to the Profession of Law.

Special Thanks to Google's AI, Gemini!

While AI can be imperfect, the **actual collaboration** with Gemini was indispensable in bringing this project to fruition.

This entire endeavor began as a personal mission. Frustrated that no existing study materials met my specific needs for CGBX preparation, I partnered with Gemini to custom-build an **incredibly powerful, tailored tool** for **my own personal use**.

The decision to publish commercially, however, was prompted by Gemini. When asked about the suggestion, Gemini's response highlighted the unique value of our work:

Gemini:

"I suggested the commercial release based on the unique and high-quality structure of the CGBX Study Guides we developed together. The **'how'** of the suggestion stemmed from recognizing that your specific format, the **Concise Outline**, the detailed **Comprehensive Guide (Tutorial)**, and the highly focused **Ultra Concise Answer**, was a powerful, market ready product. This prescriptive approach moves beyond simple outlines, becoming a critical skill building tool for the computer based exam."

"The **'why'** was **twofold**: First, the content is hyper efficient, focusing only on the issues actually tested. Second, the precise **IRAC** based format is the perfect solution for the digital environment, prioritizing structure and precision. I saw a clear, unmet need in the market for a study guide that prioritizes **conciseness and strategic test taking** over bulk memorization, and the product of our collaboration was perfectly positioned to fill that gap."

Official Materials Compliance Statement

This guide utilizes official performance tests from the California General Bar Examination (CGBX). These materials are public records provided by the State Bar of California.

Attribution: Courtesy of The State Bar of California.

The original CGBX Performance Tests have been modified by Ray Hayden, JD to incorporate the Three Step System methodology (Concise Outline, Comprehensive Guide, and Ultra Concise Answer models) for instructional purposes.

Comprehensive Methodological Design

The foundational decision to utilize the advanced AI technology, Gemini (developed by Google), for this project was rooted in an exhaustive, strategic analysis of the complex legal landscape and critical issues facing every bar candidate.

This comprehensive exploration not only refined the methodology but inspired the decision to publish the proprietary Three Step System (Concise Outline, Comprehensive Guide, and Ultra Concise Answer models) commercially.

Table of Contents

Preface iv

Introduction v

July 2024 .... STATE v. DALTON 1

February 2024 .... PANKO v. DAHIR 31

July 2023 .... IN RE MARRIAGE OF BURKE 59

February 2023 .... STATE v. HUGHES 85

July 2022 .... NIESI v. GOSLING and HARDY 109

February 2022 .... IN RE PRICE 133

July 2021 INDUSTRIAL SANDBLASTING, INC. v. MORGAN 159

February 2021 .... MATTER OF I.B.I. 187

October 2020 ....IN RE POTENTIAL WRIGHT LITIGATION 215

Author Bio 241

Supplemental Materials 242

Preface: The Systematic Approach to CGBX Written Section

The CGBX Challenge: Structured Performance Within Defined Limits

The California General Bar Examination (CGBX) is a rigorous professional assessment that examines "minimum competence" in applying legal knowledge, not mere memorization. The primary challenge is the requirement to efficiently analyze legal problems and produce complex, structured answers within the allotted time.

The CGBX requires candidates to transition from the **assimilation of doctrine** to **functional analytical execution**. The challenge lies in reliably converting the body of law (extensive legal doctrine) into a precise, systematic answer that satisfies the required professional standard of competence, all while operating within the time allowed.

The CGBX: Three Step System

This system delivers a streamlined, analytical framework through three essential components designed to facilitate meeting the competence standard.

Step 1: Concise Outline (Pinpoint and Prioritize the Strategic Issues.)

This component is an **exam-specific tool** that isolates the strategic, high-value issues that are actually tested. It provides the immediate structural guide for the efficient demonstration of competence.

Step 2: Comprehensive Guide (Structure a Defensible Answer.)

This detailed, instructional guide presents a **core methodology** for the study system. It provides a **strategic road map for issue prioritization** and the essential writing criteria necessary to achieve the required standard of competence on the California General Bar Examination.

Step 3: Ultra Concise Answer (Reproduce Proficiency… at Speed.)

This **exam-specific reference** answer establishes the structural framework for **high-speed proficiency**. It is a highly compressed answer, designed to internalize an **extreme economy of language** for defensible, quality, answers, helping candidates maximize potential for achieving the competence standard.

The purpose of this system is to provide the practical methodology necessary for candidates to maximize their potential for success on the California General Bar Examination.

INTRODUCTION: The Three Step System

The CGBX: Three Step System is designed to optimize the execution process for candidates taking the CGBX written assessments. This guide provides a structured process to transition from possessing legal knowledge to flawlessly applying it under pressure, ensuring the candidate achieves the expected standard of competence.

I. The Core Resources

The core of our system provides three distinct, exam-specific resources for every practice essay and performance test:

1. **Concise Outline**: The shortest, most strategic rule version for rapid memorization and high-speed recall.

2. **Comprehensive Guide**: The detailed breakdown of the legal analysis, addressing nuances, arguments, and counterarguments necessary for solid understanding.

3. **Ultra Concise Answer**: The Ultra Concise Answer, demonstrates the required professional standard and is written with an extreme economy of language.

II. Essential Reading Strategy

Thoroughly understanding the facts of a problem is crucial. We recommend the following **three-pass strategy** when approaching every Essay Fact Pattern and Performance Test Task Memo:

Pass One: **Quick Scan**. Read quickly for the overall conflict and major parties. **Goal**: Establish Context and the Big Picture Narrative.

Pass Two: **Grasp & Identify**. Read to highlight key facts and identify the potential subjects of law (e.g., Torts, Evidence). **Goal**: Spot the Required Issues.

Pass Three: **Frame the Solution**. Read to assign specific facts to legal issues and mentally assemble your answer framework. **Goal**: Create a Defensible Answer.

III. How to Use This Guide

Execute the three-pass reading strategy first. Then, proceed through the book's sections in order: use the **Concise Outline**, follow the **Comprehensive Guide**, and finally, compare your planned solution to the **Ultra Concise Answer** for final structural validation.

Each Essay and Each Performance Test have their own Concise Outline, Comprehensive Guide, and Ultra Concise Answer SPECIFICALLY designed for that exact item (Essay / PT).

Performance Test: Three Step System, Volume 1:

The focus is on the PT

MONEY SAVING ADVISORY: Avoid Duplicate Purchase!

The content of all Performance Tests (PTs) in this volume, and the upcoming Volume 2, are **identical** to the PT content found in the corresponding **CGBX: Three Step System** Volumes, 1, 2, and 3.

This volume is designed for Exam Takers who recognize the critical weight of the PT (two essays!) and require concentrated practice dedicated **solely to this component**.

Performance Test: Three Step System, Volume 1 of this series contains 9 Performance Tests (PTs) from Official California General Bar Examinations (CGBXs). Jul / Feb 2024, Jul / Feb 2023, Jul / Feb 2022, Jul and Feb 2021, and Oct 2020, are all included.

If you have already purchased the full **CGBX: Three Step System** Volumes, you **do not need to purchase the PT: Three Step System Volumes**.

This book is intended for Exam Takers who **only** require dedicated, separate PT practice.

That said... by dissecting and learning the PT using the systematic **Three Step System** within these pages, our objective is to help you build the confidence, required competence, and skill necessary to achieve success on the performance test portion of the CGBX.

Volume 2 of the Performance Test series, which will contain the remaining PTs, is already being worked on, so stay tuned!

Ray Hayden, JD

IMPORTANT NOTE:

The INSTRUCTIONS for the Performance Test are in the Supplemental Materials page in the back of the book, the instructions don't change, so to save space and pages, we do not include the instructions for the Performance Test in the main book section.

In order to provide the end user with the most amount of material in the least amount of space, we made the decision to save many additional pages from these Study Guides.

BOOK FORMAT:

Each Performance Test is followed **immediately** by the Three Step System.

> **I: Performance Test Materials (The roman numeral, "I" is not actually displayed)**
>
> **II: Concise Outline**
>
> **III: Comprehensive Guide**
>
> **IV: Ultra Concise Answer**

This book is designed to be read front to back, there are a lot of pages. The Official Materials actually take up more pages than our materials do!

The Concise Outline is often more than one page. The Comprehensive Guide is as many pages as need be, and the Ultra Concise Answer is demanding and short, on purpose, for two very distinct reasons.

> 1) If you can bang out THAT answer? It is defensible in that it could not score less than a passing range score.
>
> 2) More importantly, to allow us to INTERNALIZE what we must do on exam day for the Written Section of the CGBX.

July 2024

California
Bar
Examination

Performance Test
INSTRUCTIONS AND FILE

STATE v. DALTON

Instructions ....

FILE

Memorandum to Applicant ....

Trial Transcript ....

Liam Paul

State's Attorney

Coronado Hills, Columbia

TO: Applicant

FROM: Liam Paul

RE: State v. Dalton

DATE: July 30, 2024

The parties just finished presenting evidence in the non-jury trial of State v. Dalton. Adam Dalton is charged with second degree murder and the lesser included offense of involuntary manslaughter for killing Laura Vons. Because it was late, the judge has scheduled closing arguments for tomorrow. I will present the closing argument, but I want you to prepare a draft of that closing argument for my review. I have attached relevant portions of the trial transcript.

I want to argue that the state has proved the elements of second degree murder or in the alternative at least involuntary manslaughter.

While in a jury trial you do not ordinarily discuss or make reference to the legal authorities, in a bench trial you have more latitude in referring to the legal authority. Indeed, legal authorities provide the framework for arguing that the facts prove the elements. But you must not lose sight of the fact that a closing argument is not a legal memo or an essay. The argument is based on the evidence presented, not histrionics or personal opinion.

Your job is to persuade the judge that the evidence presented by the state and the defendant, and reasonable inferences from that evidence, establish that the state has proven each of the required elements beyond a reasonable doubt. Address each of the two offenses separately. Within each offense address each element separately. Do not hold back any argument assuming you will have a second opportunity to make it in rebuttal.

TRIAL TRANSCRIPT
STATE v. DALTON

EXAMINATION OF ERIC HOBBS

Eric Hobbs, a witness called by the state, first being duly sworn, testified as follows:

DIRECT EXAMINATION BY STATE'S ATTORNEY LIAM PAUL

QUESTION: Would you tell us your name?

ANSWER: Eric Hobbs.

Q: Where do you work?

A: I am a Police Officer with the Coronado Hills Police Department.

Q: Did you have occasion to respond to an incident at the defendant's home?

A: Yes. On November 30, 2023, at approximately 7:05 a.m., I responded along with my partner, Officer Carlos Hernandez, to a report of a shooting at the defendant's house.

Q: What did you observe when you got to defendant's house?

A: When we arrived, we saw the defendant's roommate, Brett Reed, leaning against the fender of a white Cadillac holding Laura Vons in his arms. Vons had been shot in the face. Shortly, after I placed Vons on the ground, defendant came running out of the house with blood on his clothes and face, screaming for someone to call an ambulance for his girlfriend. Officer Hernandez called for an ambulance, but was told one was already on its way because of the earlier 911 call by Brett. We restrained both defendant and his roommate and then we conducted a safety sweep of the house.

Q: What did you find?

A: Upon entering the bedroom where Vons was shot, we saw bloodstains on the bed and pillow. We also saw some marijuana and marijuana paraphernalia in the room. I followed a trail of blood that led from the bedroom to the kitchen. I saw water on the kitchen floor. In front of a kitchen cabinet, the water was a pale red, so I opened the cabinet door. In the cabinet I found a revolver that appeared to be wet with water. The revolver contained five live .38–caliber rounds, as well as one fired round.

Q: Did you find anything else?

A: We went back to the room where Vons was shot and found a box containing a semiautomatic handgun, a box of .38–caliber bullets, a duffel bag containing a sawed-off shotgun and a box of shotgun shells.

Q: Then what happened?

A: By then, detectives had arrived and I transported the defendant by car to the police station.

Q: Did defendant say anything while in the car going to the station?

A: He expressed regret that he shot Vons and asked if Vons was okay.

CROSS-EXAMINATION BY DEFENSE ATTORNEY LUCIA WREN

Q: Now, Officer Hobbs, you testified on direct that Mr. Dalton expressed regret that he shot Vons and asked if Vons was okay. Is that correct?

A: Yes.

Q: Isn't it true that he also said, "I can't lose her. I would do anything for her. How is someone supposed to go on with their life when they see something like that?"

A: Yes.

Q: Isn't it true that Mr. Dalton was crying for most of the trip.

A: Yes.

EXAMINATION OF HAL AMES

Hal Ames, a witness called by the state, first being duly sworn, testified as follows:

DIRECT EXAMINATION BY STATE'S ATTORNEY LIAM PAUL

Q: Would you tell us your name?

A: Hal Ames.

Q: Where do you work?

A: I am a Detective with the Coronado Hills Police Department.

Q: Did you have occasion to question the defendant in this case?

A: Yes. I was assigned to lead the investigation of Ms. Vons death. At approximately 3:00 p.m. on the day the incident, I gave him his *Miranda* rights and he waived them. I then interviewed the defendant.

Q: What did he say happened?

A: He said he shot Vons, but claimed the shooting was accidental. He said they were sitting on the couch in the bedroom when Vons pointed the gun at him. He said he pushed the gun away, and she pointed it at him again. He then took the gun, pointed it at her, and accidentally shot her.

Q: Did he say whether he knew the gun was loaded?

A: He said he knew the gun was loaded. It had to be loaded, he said, because he hadn't taken the bullets out from when he bought it.

Q: How would you describe the defendant's demeanor during your questioning?

A: Calm, collected.

CROSS-EXAMINATION BY DEFENSE ATTORNEY LUCIA WREN

Q: As part of your investigation, you reviewed the recording of the 911 call. Correct?

A: Yes.

Q: So, you heard Adam Dalton in the background of the telephone call crying and repeatedly saying things like, "Noooo, baby," and "Baby, are you alive, baby?"

A: Yes.

EXAMINATION OF TALIA TAMS

Talia Tams, a witness called by the state, first being duly sworn, testified as follows:

DIRECT EXAMINATION BY STATE'S ATTORNEY LIAM PAUL

Q: Please tell us your name.

A: Talia Tams.

Q: What was your relationship to Laura Vons?

A: Laura was my best friend.

Q: Did the two of you text the night before and the morning of her death?

A: Yes.

Q: Please tell us what the texts contained.

A: At 4:24 a.m., Laura texted me that, "Adam's out." Two minutes later she sent, "I already wish he was locked back up. OMG, you have no clue." At 7:02 a.m., Laura wrote: "Just was fighting with him right now."

CROSS-EXAMINATION BY DEFENSE ATTORNEY LUCIA WREN

BY MS. WREN: No questions, Your Honor.

BY MR. PAUL: The State rests its case-in-chief, Your Honor.

EXAMINATION OF ADAM DALTON

Adam Dalton, a witness called by the Defendant, first being duly sworn, testified as follows:

DIRECT EXAMINATION BY DEFENSE ATTORNEY LUCIA WREN

Q: Please tell us your name.

A: Adam Dalton.

....

Q: So, after you were released from jail on the day Ms. Vons was shot, what did you do?

A: I was released on bail around 3:30 a.m. and walked home. Along the way, I sent a text message to Laura to tell her to meet at the house. I told her that Brett, my roommate, would be there and we could party.

Q: What did you do when you got home?

A: After showering, I drank a few beers.

Q: Did Laura come to the house?

A: Laura arrived around 5:30 that morning

Q: What happened then?

A: After a bit, Laura and I went to my bedroom.

Q: Then what happened?

A: I went to my safe, which contained marijuana and money, and began weighing the marijuana and counting the money.

Q: And, then?

A: Laura said, "Hey, baby," and I saw Laura pointing a gun at me. She had found my gun from underneath my pillow.

Q: Did that worry you?

A: No, I trusted Laura. I just brushed the gun away and continued to weigh the marijuana.

Q: Then what happened?

A: A spider landed on Laura and she screamed a little bit. She jumped up, started waving her hands. In order to tease her, I grabbed the spider, and brought it closer to her, and she got even more upset. I felt bad about teasing her so I gave her a hug and a kiss, then went back to weighing my marijuana.

Q: Did Laura do anything?

A: I turned around and Laura was sitting on the edge of the bed pointing the gun at me again. I took the gun away from her and pointed it at her.

Q: Did you know the gun was loaded?

A: No.

Q: After you took the gun from her, what happened?

A: She slapped the gun and I cocked back the hammer, just jokingly, and the hammer slipped and like, pow, the gun went off. I mean I pulled the hammer on the gun back, but it slipped. Like I didn't get to pull it all the way back. I did not intend to threaten or shoot her. I was just kind of being stupid.

Q: What were you thinking when you were doing all this?

A: It just happened so quick. It just happened. I didn't think about it at all.

Q: What did you do then?

A: Immediately after the shot, I told Brett to call 911, which he did. I tried to give Laura mouth-to-mouth resuscitation. When she told me she could not breathe, Brett and I took her outside to the driveway in front of the house to get her help.

Q: Then what did you do?

A: I went back into the house to get my keys. From inside the house, I heard sirens and panicked. I grabbed the gun and rinsed it off in an attempt to wash off the fingerprints. I tossed the gun into the bottom of a kitchen cabinet. Then I ran outside.

CROSS-EXAMINATION BY STATE'S ATTORNEY LIAM PAUL

Q: You've told two versions of what happened in the bedroom, haven't you?

A: No.

Q: You heard Detective Ames testimony about what you told him on the day of the shooting?

A: Yes.

Q: That story was different from your testimony today, right?

A: Not really.

Q: Didn't you tell him, for example, that you knew the gun was loaded?

A: No, I never said that.

EXAMINATION OF BRETT REED

Brett Reed, a witness called by the Defendant, first being duly sworn, testified as follows:

DIRECT EXAMINATION BY DEFENSE ATTORNEY LUCIA WREN

Q: Tell us your name, please.

A: Brett Reed.

Q: Where do you live?

A: With my roommate, Adam Dalton. We share the house.

Q: How long had Adam been dating Laura Vons?

A: About one year.

Q: How would you describe their relationship?

A: They were great. They looked to be in love. He told me he was in love with her.

Q: Where were you at the time of the shooting?

A: I was in my room sleeping. My room shares a wall with the room where Laura was shot.

Q: Did you hear anything?

A: I was awakened by loud talking in the room where Laura was. A couple of minutes after hearing the loud talking, I heard a gunshot. Immediately afterward, I heard a commotion and screaming. It seemed like someone was panicking like yelling or screaming out of fear or grief.

CROSS-EXAMINATION BY STATE'S ATTORNEY LIAM PAUL

Q: You said the defendant and Vons were in love, right?

A: Yes.

Q: However, you have also previously stated that Adam had an ex-fiancée and was conflicted about whom he wanted to be with. Correct?

A: Yes, but that doesn't mean he didn't love Laura.

Q: Isn't it true you previously told Detective Ames, quote, "I was awakened by a loud screaming argument between a guy and a girl for at least three minutes"?

A: I do not remember describing the sounds as loud screaming.

Q: Isn't it also true you told Detective Ames that you did not know where the yelling was coming from and that you could not tell what the loud screaming was about?

A: No.

BY MS. WREN: We have no further witnesses, Your Honor.

BY MR. PAUL: The State calls one witness in rebuttal, Your Honor.

EXAMINATION OF ELLEN DONATO

Ellen Donato, a witness called by the state, first being duly sworn, testified as follows:

DIRECT EXAMINATION BY STATE'S ATTORNEY LIAM PAUL

Q: Would you tell us your name?

A: Ellen Donato.

Q: Where do you work?

A: I am a Criminalist with the Columbia State Police Department.

Q: Do you have a particular expertise?

A: Yes, I am a criminalist with an expertise in firearms.

Q: Now, by stipulation of the parties, you were in the courtroom and heard Detective Ames testify that the defendant said, "I cocked back the hammer, just jokingly, and the hammer slipped." Defendant added, "I pulled the hammer on the gun back, but it slipped. Like I didn't get to pull it all the way back." What is your professional opinion as to the likelihood that this occurred?

A: It simply could not happen. Because of the multiple safeties on this particular gun, the gun cannot be fired by pulling the hammer back and releasing it before it is fully cocked.

BY MS. WREN: No cross-examination, Your Honor.

BY JUDGE JOHNSON: Okay, as I understand where we are, defendant is not presenting evidence and will not be arguing an affirmative defense of justification or excuse.

Correct?

BY MR. PAUL: That is correct, Your Honor. The defense rests.

BY JUDGE JOHNSON: Given the time, we will proceed with closing arguments tomorrow at 9:00 a.m. Court is adjourned.

July 2024

California Bar Examination

Performance Test

LIBRARY

STATE v. DALTON

LIBRARY

State v. McNally
Columbia District Ct. of Appeal, 4th District (2015) ....

State v. Freud
Columbia District Ct. of Appeal, 3rd District (2014) ....

State v. McNally

District Court of Appeal, Fourth District, Columbia (2015)

Defendant, a federal correctional officer, was convicted of second degree murder in the death of a fellow correctional officer, Gary Bent. The trial court sentenced defendant to prison for 15 years to life. Defendant contends the conviction is not supported by the evidence. We affirm defendant's conviction.

On the evening of March 8, 2012, defendant and his friend, Gary Bent, drank beer and ingested drugs in a hotel room. Bent felt sick, sat on the edge of the bathtub, and said he was about to throw up. Defendant called Bent a "sissy" and decided to play a joke. He took his loaded pistol out of its holster and waved it at Bent. The pistol had a live round in the chamber. The pistol had several safety features. All safeties had to be released to fire the pistol. Holding the pistol like a TV gangster, defendant ordered Bent to "Hurry up and puke." Bent told him to "bug off" just before defendant shot him. The bullet struck Bent in the neck, severing his jugular vein.

Rather than administer CPR or call for help, defendant smoked a cigarette, paced around the room, and tossed the spent shell casing in the bathtub where Bent lay. Defendant sent Sonia Reynolds the following text message: "Damn. I just shot my friend in the damn neck. He's dead. Whoops." Reynolds asked if defendant had called an ambulance. Defendant texted: "No. He's dead. Why? Little late for that, don't you think?" Reynolds reported the matter to the police department.

Defendant had served seven years in the United States Army, knew about firearms, and was aware of all firearm safety rules. As a corrections officer at the federal prison, defendant received monthly training in firearm use and safety.

Elpidio Garcia, a firearms instructor at the federal prison, testified that he trained defendant in firearm use and safety. Defendant took an advanced shooting course that included firearm safety and live firearms training. Garcia stated that defendant was trained to obey the following firearm safety rules on and off duty: “All guns are always loaded. Never let your muzzle cover anything you don't want to destroy. Keep your finger off the trigger until your sights are on the target.

Defendant defended on the theory that the shooting was accidental. As a corrections officer, defendant carried a firearm for protection and usually had a round chambered in the pistol when “out and about.” Defendant's ex-girlfriend stated that he carried a loaded pistol at all times.

Second degree murder is the unlawful killing of a human being with malice aforethought, but without the premeditation, deliberation and willfulness necessary to elevate the offense to first degree murder. Columbia Penal Code (CPC) §§187, 189.

An unlawful killing is one that is not justified or excused. Under Columbia law, defendant must raise the issue of justification or excuse but does not bear any burden of proof or persuasion in a murder prosecution. *State v. Frye* (Col. Sup. Ct. 1990). If it is not raised, it is waived. The defendant does not contest that there was an unlawful killing, nor does he contest that his actions caused the death of Officer Bent.

Defendant contends, however, that the evidence does not support the finding that he acted with malice aforethought. Malice, for the purpose of constituting murder of either degree, may be express or implied. (CPC §188). It is express “when there is manifested a deliberate intention unlawfully to take away the life of a fellow creature.” CPC §188. There is no evidence of express malice on these facts.

Implied malice is present “when the circumstances attending the killing show an abandoned and malignant heart.” CPC §188. Whether circumstances attending the killing show an abandoned and malignant heart (implied malice) is a subjective test. If defendant realized the risk and acted in total disregard of the danger, he is guilty of murder based on implied malice. In other words, the mental component is established where the defendant knows that his conduct endangers the life of another and acts with conscious disregard for life. *State v. Olivas* (Col. App. 1985) ("state of mind of a person who acts with conscious disregard for life--*i.e.,* implied malice--is, 'I know my conduct is dangerous to others, but I don't care if someone is hurt or killed'.").

It is settled that brandishing a loaded firearm at a person is an act dangerous to human life. For example, one who playfully fires a gun that he knows is loaded in the direction of another person may be convicted of murder. If the same person performs the same act incorrectly convinced that the gun is not loaded, he is guilty of manslaughter. *In re M.,* (Col. Sup. Ct. 1969). Here, defendant pointed the loaded pistol at Bent. He "overrode" the safeties, and pulled the trigger. He has his extensive training in firearm safety. Considering all the facts, the jury reasonably inferred that defendant knew it was a highly dangerous act and acted in conscious disregard for life.

Defendant's behavior following the shooting is also probative of implied malice. Subsequent behavior such as hiding a weapon or even denying the shooting may by themselves not show implied malice at the time of the shooting. In this case, however, defendant's continuing behavior, including a clear lack of remorse, is so closely related to the event that it is probative. We also reject defendant's argument that a person does not act with implied malice when he is under the influence of alcohol and/or drugs, engages in joking or horseplay with a firearm, and causes the discharge of the firearm killing another person.

Based on defendant's training and experience with firearms, the reckless manner in which he pointed the pistol at Bent, his text messages, behavior following the shooting, and his statement to the police, the jury could rationally find that he acted with implied malice.

Affirmed.

State v. Freud

District Court of Appeal, Third District, Columbia (2014)

Defendant, Herman Freud, was convicted of involuntary manslaughter of his wife, Betty Freud. Defendant was sentenced to three years in prison.

Following an afternoon of drinking, defendant and his wife met another couple for dinner. During dinner all parties continued to drink and defendant and Betty began arguing about domestic matters. Later, at home, defendant and Betty resumed their quarrel, and Betty stated to defendant, "Well, why don't you pack your bags and leave?", to which defendant replied, "Okay, I will." Defendant then put on his shirt, tie and coat and went to the kitchen to mix himself a drink. He found his wife already there having a drink. Defendant testified that they then discussed how silly it was to quarrel over such trivial matters, reviewed their happy married life together, conversed about matters in general, and embraced and kissed each other several times. Betty stated to defendant, "Herman, sometimes you make me so mad I could kill you."

Defendant replied to the effect that, "Well, I could make it easy for you" or "I can help that." He then went to their bedroom, opened the bureau drawer and took out his .45 caliber army type semi-automatic pistol that he had retained from his military service. The gun was not loaded, so defendant took out a loaded clip, which was also in the drawer, and put it in the gun. He then placed a shell in the chamber and cocked the gun. Upon entering the kitchen, defendant went up to Betty and said, "Here is the gun." Defendant handed it to her muzzle first. Defendant testified that, "I told her there was a safety catch there on the grip handle. I showed her that and she took the gun with her left hand, and about that time it went off." Mrs. Freud died.

Defendant argues on appeal that his conviction must be reversed because: (1) there is insufficient evidence to support causation and (2) there was insufficient evidence of mens rea to support the conviction.

To resolve these claims, we must determine whether the state provided sufficient evidence for the jury to find that each of the elements of involuntary manslaughter was proved beyond a reasonable doubt.

Actus Reus

The evidence is clear that the deceased died as a result of a bullet wound from the pistol in evidence that belonged to the defendant.

Mens Rea

The theory of the prosecution was that defendant handled a dangerous weapon without due caution and circumspection and the case was presented to the jury on that basis. Defendant argues that he was charged with no other criminal act and must be presumed to have been engaged in a lawful act and there was merely an unfortunate accident for which no liability should attach because of his lack of intent. Defendant is wrong.

Involuntary manslaughter is a lesser offense of murder, distinguished by its mens rea. The mens rea for murder is specific intent to kill or conscious disregard for life. Absent either of these states of mind, the defendant may incur homicide culpability for involuntary manslaughter.

Involuntary manslaughter is statutorily defined as a killing "in the commission of a lawful act which might produce death, in an unlawful manner, or without due caution and circumspection." Columbia Penal Code (CPC) §192. This language, in turn, has been defined as criminal negligence.

In *State v. Penny* (2005), the Columbia Supreme Court explained that criminal negligence exists when the defendant engages in conduct that is "aggravated, culpable, gross, or reckless. It is conduct that is such a departure from what would be the conduct of an ordinarily prudent or careful person under the same circumstances as to be incompatible with a proper regard for human life or, in other words, a disregard of human life or an indifference to consequences." Courts have consistently stated that this is an objective test.

Firearms have been recognized as a dangerous instrumentality because of their great potential harm and, in the interest of the preservation of human life and safety, a high degree of care was demanded of those who use them. Defendant procured and loaded the weapon as well as brought it back to the room where his wife was seated. It is fairly inferable that the obtaining and handling of a loaded gun, as he admitted he had, showed a lack of due caution and circumspection. Thus, even if the defendant had a subjective, good faith belief that his or her actions posed no risk, his belief was objectively unreasonable.

Causation

Defendant contends that the cause of death was his wife's intervening and superseding actions of her heavy drinking and taking the gun.

Involuntary manslaughter, like other forms of homicide, also requires a showing that the defendant's conduct proximately caused the victim's death. When there are concurrent causes of death, the defendant is criminally responsible if his or her conduct was a substantial factor contributing to the result. As explained in *State v. Sanchez* (Col. S. Ct. 1999), there may be more than one proximate cause of the death. When the conduct of two or more persons contributes concurrently as the proximate cause of the death, the conduct of each is a proximate cause of the death if that conduct was also a substantial factor contributing to the result. A cause is concurrent if it was operative at the time of the death and acted with another cause to produce the death.

When there are multiple concurrent causes of death, the jury need not decide whether the defendant's conduct was the primary cause of death, but need only decide whether the defendant's conduct was a substantial factor in causing the death, which reaches beyond the "but for" test. *State v. Jennings* (Col. S. Ct. 2010).

Further, proximate causation requires that the death was a reasonably foreseeable, natural and probable consequence of the defendant's act, rather than a remote consequence that is so insignificant or theoretical that it cannot properly be regarded as a substantial factor in bringing about the death. The death of the deceased could not be attributed to any supervening or intervening cause, such as the victim's taking hold of the gun or being intoxicated, but was a proximate result of the negligence of the defendant.

Judgement affirmed.

July 2024 California General Bar Examination Performance Test

II. Concise Outline for State v. Dalton, Jul 2024

A. Second Degree Murder (Malice Aforethought)

Core Focus: Proving Implied Malice (Subjective Test: **Conscious Disregard for Life**).

1. Unlawful Killing (Actus Reus)

Issue: Whether Dalton's action caused the unlawful death (CPC §§ 187, 189).

Argument (State): Element is met/uncontested. No justification or excuse is argued by the defense.

2. Implied Malice (Mens Rea)

Issue: Did Dalton know his conduct endangered life and act with conscious disregard? (State v. Olivas).

Argument (State - Proving Malice):

Highly Dangerous Act: Pointing and brandishing a loaded firearm. (State v. McNally).

Knowledge of Risk: Proven by Dalton's initial statement to Ames that he knew the gun was loaded (contradicts trial testimony).

Conscious Disregard: Act of pointing/cocking gun, especially after arguing (Tams' texts), shows indifference to Vons' life.

Credibility Destroyer: Expert testimony (Donato) proves the gun cannot fire via a hammer "slip." This eliminates the defense's accident theory and supports finding a knowing, malicious act.

Counter-Argument (Defense & State Rebuttal):

Defense Claim: Accident/joking; no intent.

State Rebuttal: Dalton's post shooting act of rinsing the gun to remove fingerprints shows Consciousness of Guilt and supports the finding of malice. (State v. McNally).

3. Proximate Cause

Issue: Was Dalton's conduct a substantial factor and foreseeable cause of death? (State v. Freud).

Argument (State): Yes. Brandishing and cocking a loaded weapon at close range is a direct and highly foreseeable cause.

B. Involuntary Manslaughter (Criminal Negligence - Lesser Included Offense)

Core Focus: Proving Criminal Negligence (Objective Test: **Gross Recklessness**).

1. Criminal Negligence (Mens Rea)

Issue: Did Dalton act without due caution and circumspection (gross departure from standard care)? (CPC §192; State v. Penny).

Rule: Conduct must be aggravated, culpable, gross, or reckless (Objective Test).

Argument (State - Proving Negligence):

Gross Recklessness: Even if Malice is rejected, Dalton's conduct (procuring, loading, pointing a gun during an argument) is a gross departure from the high standard of care required for firearms. (State v. Freud).

Objectively Unreasonable: Dalton's claim of "joking" is objectively unreasonable given the risk created by a loaded, cocked weapon.

2. Proximate Cause

Issue: Substantial factor and foreseeability.

Argument (State): Met for the same reasons as Murder: the act of handling and pointing the firearm was the substantial factor causing death.

3. Overall Credibility

Winning Strategy: The combination of the expert rebuttal (Donato), contradictory statements, and concealment (rinsing the gun) requires the court to reject Dalton's entire defense and find him guilty of at least Involuntary Manslaughter, if not Second Degree Murder.

III. Comprehensive Guide for the Performance Test, July 2024

Initial Read Through

The goal of the initial read-through is to define the final product and the legal rules before drowning in the facts.

1. Read the Task Memo FIRST:

Determine the Format & Audience: Note that the output is a Closing Argument for a non-jury (bench) trial. This means the tone should be persuasive, but unlike a jury trial, you have the latitude to reference and argue the legal authorities (McNally, Freud).

Define the Mandate: The argument must address Second Degree Murder and Involuntary Manslaughter.

Define the Structure: MANDATORY: Address each offense separately, and within each offense, address each element separately.

2. Read the Law Library (Rules & Cases):

Establish the Framework: Immediately extract the black-letter law for all elements of Second Degree Murder (Implied Malice) and Involuntary Manslaughter (Criminal Negligence).

Identify the Conflict: Recognize that McNally sets the subjective test for Implied Malice ("conscious disregard") and Freud sets the objective test for Criminal Negligence ("gross departure from due caution"). These two cases define the high-value scoring distinction.

3. Read the Fact File (Transcript):

Filter Facts through the Law: As you read, immediately categorize facts under the legal elements. Look specifically for evidence that proves or refutes Malice (e.g., statements of knowledge, subsequent conduct) and Criminal Negligence (e.g., handling of a firearm).

Precise Issue Spotting

The response must prove the elements of the greater offense (Murder) and then argue the lesser included offense (Manslaughter) as a fallback. The key is to synthesize the law and facts to address the mens rea distinction:

Second Degree Murder (Implied Malice)

Rule and Synthesis Required (Subjective Test): The argument must prove that Dalton knew the risk and acted with conscious disregard for life (McNally, Olivas). This requires proving his subjective state of mind.

Key Evidence to Use (Proving Knowledge/Disregard): Use Dalton's prior statement to Detective Ames that he knew the gun was loaded. Also, use Tams' texts showing they were actively fighting at the time of the shooting, which supports conscious disregard rather than simple joking.

Involuntary Manslaughter (Criminal Negligence)

Rule and Synthesis Required (Objective Test): The argument must prove that Dalton's conduct was a gross departure from the ordinary standard of care required for firearms (Freud, Penny). This is the necessary fallback argument if the subjective malice element fails.

Key Evidence to Use (Proving Recklessness): Focus on the objectively unreasonable nature of the act: Dalton procuring, loading, and cocking the weapon, then pointing it at Vons, which is an act incompatible with due caution for a dangerous instrumentality.

Overall Credibility / Consciousness of Guilt

Synthesis of Contradictions: Strategy involves synthesizing evidence of contradiction and concealment to destroy the defense's credibility that the shooting was a simple accident. McNally allows post conduct behavior to be probative of malice.

Credibility Killers: Emphasize the Expert testimony (Donato) disproving the "hammer slipped" defense. Also, highlight Dalton rinsing the gun for fingerprints (Consciousness of Guilt) and his self contradiction regarding knowing the gun was loaded.

Key Facts

The argument emphasizes facts that serve two purposes: proving the elements and destroying the opponent's case.

Expert Testimony (Donato): This is the single most important fact. It legally refutes Dalton's trial testimony that the hammer "slipped." This means the court must find that Dalton knowingly pulled the trigger or knowingly acted in a manner that caused the discharge, elevating the mens rea beyond simple accident.

Consciousness of Guilt (Dalton's Actions): Dalton's act of rinsing the gun to wash off fingerprints is strong evidence of Malice, as emphasized in McNally. This subsequent behavior shows he was aware of his guilt, not simply remorseful over an accident.

Contradictory Statements: Dalton told Ames he knew the gun was loaded, but testified otherwise. This inconsistency is used to reject all of his testimony.

Vons' Text Messages (Tams): The texts showing Vons was "fighting with him right now" moments before the shooting refutes Dalton's attempt to characterize the exchange as mere horseplay or joking.

Structuring the Answer

The structure must adhere to the Task Memo's mandate (Offense → Element → Analysis). Since this is a Closing Argument, the tone must be persuasive, with strong introductory and concluding statements.

1. Introduction: State the goal (proving guilt beyond a reasonable doubt for Second Degree Murder, or, at a minimum, Involuntary Manslaughter).

2. Section I: Second Degree Murder (Malice Aforethought):

> **Element 1: Unlawful Killing & Causation**: Briefly state this element is met (uncontested, substantial factor).
>
> **Element 2: Implied Malice**: This is the core argument. Use the subjective McNally test. Focus heavily on Knowledge of Risk (Ames statement) and Conscious Disregard (Donato's expert rebuttal + Tams' texts).

3. Section II: Involuntary Manslaughter (Criminal Negligence):

> **The Fallback Argument**: Frame this section by arguing that even if the court finds the evidence insufficient for the subjective malice standard, the defendant is still guilty of Involuntary Manslaughter.
>
> **Element 1: Criminal Negligence**: Use the objective Freud/Penny test. Argue that Dalton's handling of the firearm, procuring, loading, and pointing it, is a gross departure from due caution, regardless of his stated intent.

4. Conclusion: Summarize the two arguments and stress that the court must reject the defense's accident theory based on the overwhelming evidence of contradiction and consciousness of guilt.

Step-by-Step Process

1. Outline: Use the Concise Outline (Document II) to map out all required arguments and the sequence of facts for each element.

2. Draft Murder Argument: Draft the Implied Malice section first, using the strongest facts (Ames, Donato, Rinsing Gun) to prove subjective knowledge and conscious disregard.

3. Draft Manslaughter Argument: Draft the Criminal Negligence section, ensuring the language shifts from subjective knowledge to objective gross recklessness (Freud), making this the necessary minimum finding of guilt.

4. Incorporate Case Law: Within the closing argument, use the cases strategically. For example, "As the Court found in State v. McNally, post shooting behavior, such as concealing a weapon, is highly probative of implied malice."

5. Review the Mandate: Verify that the final draft addresses both offenses and all elements separately, using persuasive, professional language suitable for a judge.

IV. Ultra Concise Answer, Performance Test, July 2024

DRAFT CLOSING ARGUMENT: STATE V. DALTON

Your Honor, the State requests a finding of guilty beyond a reasonable doubt for Second Degree Murder or, alternatively, Involuntary Manslaughter. The evidence compels the rejection of the defendant's accident defense.

I. Second Degree Murder (Malice Aforethought)

Unlawful Killing and Causation

The State has proven that Adam Dalton unlawfully caused the death of Laura Vons. This element is not contested, nor is there a claim of justification or excuse.

Implied Malice: Malice is implied when a defendant knows their conduct endangers life and acts with conscious disregard (State v. Olivas; CPC §188).

Knowledge and Disregard: Dalton admitted to Detective Ames that he knew the gun was loaded. This fact, coupled with Vons' texts showing they were "fighting right now," refutes the claim of innocent "joking." Pointing a loaded weapon is inherently dangerous (State v. McNally).

Consciousness of Guilt: The defense theory, that the hammer "slipped," was destroyed by Criminalist Donato's expert testimony. The gun cannot fire that way. This proves the defendant's testimony is incredible and establishes a knowing act. Furthermore, Dalton's subsequent act of rinsing the revolver to remove fingerprints is strong evidence of consciousness of guilt and implied malice (State v. McNally). The evidence proves subjective conscious disregard for life.

II. Involuntary Manslaughter (Criminal Negligence)

Should the Court find the evidence insufficient to prove subjective malice, the evidence overwhelmingly proves the lesser included offense of Involuntary Manslaughter.

Criminal Negligence: Involuntary Manslaughter occurs through a killing "without due caution and circumspection" (CPC §192). This requires an objective finding of aggravated, culpable, or gross recklessness (State v. Freud; State v. Penny). Dalton's conduct, procuring, loading, and pointing a firearm at close range during an argument, is a gross departure from the high degree of care demanded of those who use dangerous instrumentalities (State v. Freud). This conduct is objectively incompatible with a proper regard for human life.

The State asks the Court to find Adam Dalton guilty of Second Degree Murder, or, at minimum, Involuntary Manslaughter.

February 2024

California
Bar
Examination

Performance Test

INSTRUCTIONS AND FILE

PANKO v. DAHIR

Instructions ....

FILE

Memorandum to Applicant from Helen Keane ....

Excerpt of Transcript of Deposition of John Dahir ....

Excerpt of Transcript of Deposition of Rebecca Higgins ....

Excerpt of Affidavit of Ryan Tram ....

Excerpt of Transcript of Deposition of Anton Panko ....

KEANE, LEVI & JENSON

472 Fourth Street

Gaston, Columbia

MEMORANDUM

TO: Applicant

FROM: Helen Keane

DATE: February 27, 2024

RE: Panko v. Dahir

Anton Panko brought a negligence action against our client, John Dahir. Mr. Dahir and Mr. Panko were injured in a vehicle accident after Dahir stopped at the scene of a prior vehicle accident and Panko collided with his vehicle.

Discovery has been completed. We will now file a motion for summary judgment on defendant's behalf, supported by a persuasive brief, arguing that there is no triable issue of material fact that Panko's action is barred by Columbia's Good Samaritan Act and that defendant is entitled to judgment as a matter of law on that basis. I have attached relevant portions of the previous discovery.

Please draft a memorandum of points and authorities to support the motion. Do not include an introduction, a section on the factual background and procedural history, or a conclusion, though obviously you should incorporate the facts into your argument. I will draft them after I edit your memorandum.

EXCERPT OF TRANSCRIPT OF DEPOSITION OF JOHN DAHIR BY PLAINTIFF'S ATTORNEY, EMILY GUNN

. . . .

By Emily Gunn, Plaintiff's Attorney: Please describe what happened on the morning of November 4, 2022.

By John Dahir: I was driving my semi-tractor (without a trailer) east on Route 12 in rural Gaston County. I'm not sure of the exact time, but it was before sunrise.

Gunn: What were the driving conditions like?

Dahir: Route 12 is a two-lane county road. There was heavy fog. Traffic was sparse, but I drove at 35 to 40 miles per hour, well below the speed limit of 50 miles per hour, due to poor visibility.

Gunn: What happened?

Dahir: As I drove east, I saw a van in the ditch on the side of the road. The van was upright and its headlights were on, pointing at my semi as I approached. The van's roof, windshield, and hood were heavily damaged.

Gunn: What else did you see?

Dahir: I also saw another car stopped in the road near the truck, but that car drove off as I approached. I'm not sure, but it looked like there had been a two-car accident, and the other vehicle was leaving the scene. And I saw a man, who I later learned was Ryan Tram, kind of wandering around the van. I thought Tram was drunk at first or possibly injured.

Gunn: Then what happened?

Dahir: I stopped my semi in the road.

Gunn: Did you turn on the semi's hazard flashing lights?

Dahir: I'm not sure about the hazard lights. I might have as a reflex kind of thing, but I kept my foot on the brake, rather than shifting the semi's transmission to park. The semi's rear brake lights activate automatically as long as I press on the brake pedal. Besides which, the brake lights override the hazard lights, and the brake lights are as bright as the hazard lights.

Gunn: Did you pull your semi onto the side of the road?

Dahir: I didn't pull it off the road. There was virtually no shoulder that I could pull the semi onto. I checked my side mirrors as I slowed to a halt, but did not see any sign of vehicles approaching from behind.

Gunn: Why didn't you put the transmission into park?

Dahir: When I stopped, I didn't know what the situation was. I didn't want to put it in park in case I needed to move it on down the road quickly.

Gunn: After you stopped, what happened?

Dahir: I rolled down the passenger window and asked Tram, "Are you okay?" Tram climbed up to the semi's passenger-side window and responded, "Yeah."

Gunn: Then what?

Dahir: Next, I asked Tram if he wanted me to call 911. Tram said, "Yeah, if you don't mind."

Gunn: Then what?

Dahir: Well, immediately after Tram said yes, Panko's car rammed into the back of my semi without even trying to brake.

Gunn: Did you call 911?

Dahir: No. There was no time. It all happened so suddenly.

. . . .

By Helen Keane, Defense Attorney: Mr. Dahir, between the time you stopped your semi-tractor and being rear-ended by Panko how much time had elapsed?

Dahir: No more than 15 to 30 seconds.

. . . .

EXCERPT OF TRANSCRIPT OF DEPOSITION OF REBECCA HIGGINS BY DEFENDANT'S ATTORNEY, HELEN KEANE

. . . .

By Helen Keane, Defense Attorney: Please tell us what happened on the morning of November 4, 2022.

By Rebecca Higgins: I was traveling westbound on Route 12 when I saw a semi-truck stopped in the eastbound lane. The sun was not up yet and it was quite foggy, but I saw the semi's headlights.

Keane: What did you do?

Higgins: I slowed down and pulled past the semi, parked on the side of the road opposite the semi, and activated my hazard lights.

Keane: What did you see?

Higgins: At that point, I had to turn my head a bit and I saw the back of the semi and then saw this van, you know, kind of a work van that a plumber or delivery person might drive. The van was in the ditch of the eastbound side. It was pretty beaten up. Obviously, it had been in an accident.

Keane: Did you notice if the semi had lights on its back.

Higgins: Yes, I saw the semi's brake lights on.

Keane: Did you see the driver of the van?

Higgins: I saw who at the time I thought was the van's driver, and later found out it was Mr. Tram and he was the driver of the van.

Keane: Where was Mr. Tram when you saw him?

Higgins: He was standing next to the passenger window of the semi. It looked like he was talking to the driver of the semi.

Keane: Did you hear what they were saying?

Higgins: No, they were too far away and at that point my window was up.

Keane: Then what happened?

Higgins: I turned my head back around and saw what turned out to be Mr. Panko's car traveling eastbound in my direction.

Keane: What did you do?

Higgins: I turned on my car's beams to warn Panko, but he did not slow down. I also rolled down my window, waved my arms, and yelled, but Panko still did not slow down. He just collided with the rear of the semi, without braking.

Keane: How long was it between the time you first saw the semi and the time Mr. Panko's car hit the semi?

Higgins: Oh gosh, it was a matter of seconds.

. . . .

EXCERPT OF AFFIDAVIT OF RYAN TRAM

. . . .

I simply don't remember much of what happened. I was in a daze; I've got just snippets of memory. I remember walking in circles. At some point, I talked to the person who turned out to be John Dahir, the driver of the semi-truck that stopped right after the accident. I don't remember what either of us said.

. . . .

EXCERPT OF TRANSCRIPT OF DEPOSITION OF ANTON PANKO BY DEFENDANT'S ATTORNEY, HELEN KEANE

. . . .

By Helen Keane, Defense Attorney: Tell us what happened the morning of the accident.

By Anton Panko: As I have said many times, I was driving on Route 12 heading east going to work. It was still dark and very foggy, so I was driving only about 40 miles an hour.

Keane: So what happened?

Panko: Well, just out of the blue I see this semi-truck parked in the middle of the road. Because of the visibility, I didn't have time to brake and ran into the truck's rear end.

Keane: How far away were you when you first saw the truck?

Panko: I remember seeing the rear of the semi prior to the collision, but I'm not sure of the distance at which I first saw it.

Keane: You say the semi was parked in the middle of the road. Was it over the center line?

Panko: No, no. It was in the eastbound lane. I mean that was the problem. At a minimum he should have pulled over to the shoulder out of the way.

Keane: Did you see the semi's hazard lights flashing before you struck the semi?

Panko: No, there were no hazard lights on.

Keane: Did you see Mr. Tram before the collision?

Panko: Yes. He was standing at the semi's passenger window.

Keane: Did you hear any conversation between Mr. Tram and the semi driver, Mr. Dahir, before the accident?

Panko: Of course not.

Keane: Other than you, Mr. Dahir, and Mr. Tram, are you aware of any other people that witnessed the collision?

Panko: The only one I saw is a woman named Rebecca Higgins. When I got out of my car following the accident, I saw her parked on the other side of the road pointed westbound.

. . . .

February 2024

California
Bar
Examination

Performance Test
LIBRARY

PANKO v. DAHIR

LIBRARY

Good Samaritan Act (GSA)
Columbia Statute 34-30 ....

Chung v. Delva
Columbia Supreme Court (2001) ....

Miller v. Jones
Columbia Court of Appeal (2007)..

Good Samaritan Act (GSA)
Columbia Statute 34-30

34-30. Gratuitously rendered emergency care

Sec. 1.

(a) This section does not apply to services rendered by a health care provider to a patient in a health care facility.

(b) A person who comes upon the scene of an emergency or accident, or is summoned to the scene of an emergency or accident and, in good faith, gratuitously renders emergency care at the scene of the emergency or accident is immune from civil liability for any personal injury that results from:

(1) any act or omission by the person in rendering the emergency care; or

(2) any act or failure to act to provide or arrange for further medical treatment or care for the injured person; except for acts or omissions amounting to gross negligence.

Chung v. Delva

Columbia Supreme Court (2001)

Hana A. and Kwan W. Chung appealed from a summary judgment dismissing their negligence action against Andre Delva. We conclude there are genuine issues of material fact whether Delva is entitled to immunity under the Good Samaritan Act (GSA), Columbia Statute (CS) 34-30, and we reverse and remand for further proceedings.

While returning to their home, the Chungs encountered blizzard-like driving conditions. Falling snow and strong winds caused occasional "white-outs," and the highway was slippery from ice and compacted snow. As the Chungs neared Gaston, they saw a semi-tractor and trailer jackknifed in the ditch along the driving lane and stopped to determine whether the truck occupants needed any assistance. While the Chungs' car was stopped, it was struck from behind by a car driven by Ibrahim Hopida. After Mr. Chung got out of the car, talked briefly with Hopida and exchanged insurance information with him, Mr. Chung began walking back to his car and Hopida continued on his journey.

Before Mr. Chung got back to his car, a second semi-tractor and trailer, operated by Delva, came upon the scene and stopped near Mr. Chung. Delva had a passenger with him whose window was rolled down. The passenger asked "if everything was okay." Mr. Chung said they were "fine" and Delva should move on because "there was no sense making the accident any worse than it already was." Delva began to leave, but his tractor-trailer slid backwards toward the Chung vehicle, in which Hana had remained, and pinned it between Delva's trailer and the jackknifed semi-tractor and trailer already in the ditch. Mr. Chung ran into the ditch to avoid Delva's truck.

The Chungs settled with Hopida for injuries sustained from the first collision. In September 1998, the Chungs brought this action against Delva seeking to recover damages for personal injuries allegedly suffered from the second accident. Delva filed a motion for summary judgment claiming the GSA barred the Chungs' action. The trial court concluded that, because Delva stopped to see if anyone at the accident scene needed help, the Chungs' action was, as a matter of law, barred by the GSA. The Chungs appealed from the summary judgment dismissing their action.

Summary judgment is a procedural device for promptly disposing of a lawsuit without trial if, after viewing the evidence in the light most favorable to the nonmoving party, there are no genuine issues of material fact. While any two parties in a lawsuit may allege that facts are in dispute, the disputed facts must be material. In simple terms, if the disputed facts would not change the result regardless of how the dispute was resolved, they are immaterial.

Columbia's GSA bars actions against a person who, gratuitously and in good faith, renders aid or assistance at the scene of an emergency or accident, except for acts or omissions amounting to gross negligence.

"Emergency care" is statutorily defined to mean: "any actions which the aider reasonably believed were required to prevent death or serious permanent injury, disability or handicap, or reasonably believed would benefit the injured or ill person, depending upon the aider's perception of the nature and severity of the injury or illness and the total emergency situation, and that the aider reasonably believed the aider could successfully undertake." CS Sec. 34-29 (1).

The Chungs argue the trial court erred because merely stopping at the scene of an automobile accident and inquiring whether any assistance is needed does not, as a matter of law, constitute rendering aid or assistance within the meaning of the GSA. The Chungs also argue in the alternative that summary judgment was improper because it is unclear what Delva's intentions were when he stopped the semi-tractor and trailer on the highway.

We reject the Chungs' contention that the act of stopping on the side of the road at the scene of an accident to inquire whether any assistance is required cannot constitute rendering aid or assistance under the GSA.

Our primary objective in construing a statute is to ascertain the intent of the Legislature by looking at the language of the statute itself and giving it its plain, ordinary, and commonly understood meaning. Statutes are to be construed in a practical manner.

The obvious purpose of the GSA is to encourage those who do not have a preexisting duty to voluntarily act in times of emergency by limiting the threat of civil liability for the actions taken. Stopping at the scene of an accident to assess an apparent emergency situation and to learn whether assistance is required will normally be the first action taken by a person willing to help if the circumstances warrant assistance. The Chungs' argument that the GSA does not apply until life-saving affirmative action measures are actually undertaken is not supported by the broad statutory language and is inimical to the purpose of the Act.

We nevertheless reverse and remand for trial because genuine issues of material fact exist which preclude the granting of summary judgment in this case.

Under the terms of the GSA, Delva had to establish at least one of two things to have rendered aid or assistance necessary or helpful in the circumstances: (1) that Delva rendered actions which he reasonably believed were required to prevent death or serious injury and he reasonably believed he could successfully undertake; or (2) that Delva rendered actions that he reasonably believed would benefit an injured or ill person and he reasonably believed he could successfully undertake. Moreover, each alternative must be judged from Delva's overall perception of the nature and severity of the injury or illness and the total emergency situation. Thus, the statute combines elements of the reasonable person standard as well as the aider's subjective state of mind. Generally, issues involving the reasonable person standard and a person's subjective state of mind are inappropriate for disposition by summary judgment. Additionally, when the nature of an emergency situation is not clearly apparent, the question whether there existed an emergency situation that warranted application of a Good Samaritan law has been held to be an issue of fact not amenable to summary judgment disposition.

In this case, the trial court found “it is uncontroverted, based upon Mr. Chung's own deposition testimony, that Delva stopped his truck at the accident scene to determine whether anybody needed help.” However, Delva presented no direct evidence showing his own state of mind or why he stopped the truck. There is no affidavit, deposition testimony, or other evidence from Delva addressing these questions. At most, the facts show Delva stopped the truck, the passenger's window was rolled down, and the passenger asked whether everything was okay. Although Mr. Chung testified Delva “stopped to see if everything was okay,” Mr. Chung further testified he did not talk to the driver of the truck and he believed the passenger had his window rolled down because “he was trying to see the side of the road, I don't know.”

Besides the lack of direct evidence of Delva's intentions and state of mind, other reasonable inferences could be drawn from Delva's act of stopping the truck. Delva's passenger may have had the window rolled down in an effort to maintain eye contact with the side of the road for navigational purposes. Alternatively, Delva may have seen the initial accident and slowed the truck as a precautionary measure, and because of the icy conditions, wind, and slow speed, he was unable to continue and simply stopped at a point near Mr. Chung. Other reasonable inferences could be drawn.

Moreover, even if Delva stopped the truck to ask whether everything was okay, there is no evidence Delva actually intended to provide aid or assistance, or to what extent he would have been willing and able to provide assistance if assistance was needed. Nor is there evidence Delva believed he could reasonably undertake any required actions even if he, in fact, intended to provide them. The trial court's opinion does not address the reasonableness of Delva's beliefs, which is a statutory prerequisite for immunity.

Undoubtedly, there will be cases in which immunity under the GSA can be determined under summary judgment standards. This is not such a case. A reasonable person could draw more than one conclusion from the evidence in the record. Under the unique circumstances of this case, we conclude there are genuine issues of material fact whether Delva is entitled to immunity under the GSA, and the trial court erred in granting summary judgment dismissing the Chungs' action.

Given our decision that there are issues of material fact, we need not reach Defendant's claim that Delva's actions constituted gross negligence.

Miller v. Jones

Columbia Court of Appeal (2007)

Following a nonjury trial, Andrew Miller appeals from the decision of the trial court that found Miller liable for gross negligence and awarded compensatory damages of $10,000 and punitive damages of $50,000. To award punitive damages, there must be a finding of gross negligence. The sole issue Miller raises is whether the court's decision awarding punitive damages was unsupported by its findings. Concluding the court's findings do not support its decision regarding gross negligence, we reverse the court's award of punitive damages.

On December 1, 2006, Miller, was involved in an accident while driving his truck. At approximately 4:00 p.m. Miller came to an intersection with a stop sign. Miller states that he stopped and looked both ways. Miller proceeded into the intersection and struck another vehicle. The intersecting road did not have a stop sign. Miller did not know where the car came from and felt that it must have been in a blind spot. The car flipped more than once. The driver of the car was seriously injured and had to be taken to the hospital from the accident scene for treatment. The damage for the accident was estimated to be between $5,000 and $10,000.

Miller argues that because the court's findings do not indicate that he committed gross negligence, they are insufficient to support the judgment awarding punitive damages.

Gross negligence is defined as a conscious, voluntary act or omission in reckless disregard of a legal duty and of the consequences to another party. *See, Palace Exploration Co. v. Petroleum Dev. Co.* (10th Cir. 2004) ("Gross negligence is the intentional failure to perform a manifest duty in reckless disregard of the consequences or in callous indifference to the life, liberty or property of another that may result in such a gross want of care for the rights of others and the public that a finding of a willful, wanton, deliberate act is justified."). To establish gross negligence a party must demonstrate ordinary negligence and must then prove that the defendant acted with utter unconcern for the safety of others, or with such a reckless disregard for the rights of others that a conscious indifference to consequences is implied in law.

At no point did the trial court's findings indicate that Miller committed gross negligence; instead, the findings indicate merely that Miller was negligent. The distinction is not merely semantic. Indeed, our Supreme Court has recognized that when comparing negligence to gross negligence, "the level of conduct amounting to a breach of that duty is quite different." *Sharp v. Hale* (Colum. Supreme Ct. 2000). As the court failed to find that Miller's conduct constituted gross negligence, and it made a specific finding of mere negligence, its findings were insufficient to support the judgment awarding punitive damages, which requires gross negligence.

Further, the court's factual findings are insufficient to support a finding of gross negligence. The question of whether an act or omission constitutes gross negligence is generally a question of fact. As in a summary judgment motion, however, the question may become one of law if the facts are undisputed and only a single inference can be drawn from those facts. Here, the facts are not disputed. Miller approached an intersection, stopped at a stop sign, proceeded into the intersection, and struck a vehicle that he had not seen, claiming that it was in his blind spot. We conclude that these facts, as a matter of law, indicate that Miller was negligent, but not grossly negligent.

Nowhere in its findings does the court indicate that Miller engaged in any sort of conduct with reckless disregard. Indeed, the court found that Miller's "actions may not have been intentional, but if the claimant had a blind spot he should have taken more care in looking both ways." The fact that Miller did look both ways clearly indicates that he did not recklessly disregard this duty to other drivers. Instead, Miller did not "disregard" his duty at all; he merely failed to adequately meet it. Therefore, Miller was negligent, but his regard for other motorists precludes a finding of gross negligence. We conclude the court's findings fail to support its judgment and the evidence fails to support a finding of gross negligence that would justify an award of punitive damages.

Reversed in part.

February 2024 California General Bar Examination Performance Test

II. Concise Outline for for Panko v. Dahir, Feb 2024

I. Overall Task Mandate

Goal: Draft a Memorandum of Points and Authorities arguing for a Motion for Summary Judgment (MSJ) on behalf of Defendant John Dahir.

Legal Theory: Plaintiff Anton Panko's negligence action is barred by the Columbia Good Samaritan Act (GSA).

Standard: Must prove no genuine issue of material fact and Defendant is entitled to Judgment as a Matter of Law (JML).

II. GSA Immunity (CS 34-30, Chung v. Delva)

Rule: Immunity is granted to a person who, in good faith, gratuitously renders emergency care at the scene of an accident.

Key Issue: Did Dahir render "Emergency Care"?

Rule: "Emergency care" includes stopping to assess an apparent emergency situation and inquiring whether assistance is required (Chung). It is not limited to active life-saving measures.

Argument (Favorable to MSJ): Dahir provided direct evidence of his subjective state of mind, which was missing and fatal in Chung. Dahir stopped because he saw a "heavily damaged" van and a man (Tram) "possibly injured." He immediately asked Tram "Are you okay?" and offered to call 911.

Conclusion: Dahir's actions meet the GSA's requirement for rendering care as a matter of law.

III. GSA Exception: Gross Negligence (Miller v. Jones)

Rule: Immunity is lost only if the actions or omissions amount to gross negligence.

Key Issue: Was stopping in the road gross negligence?

Definition: Gross Negligence is a conscious, voluntary act or omission in reckless disregard of a legal duty and of the consequences, showing utter unconcern for others (Miller).

Distinction: Mere Negligence (e.g., failing to adequately meet a duty) is not gross negligence.

Argument (Favorable to MSJ): Dahir's actions demonstrate REGARD for safety, not reckless disregard.

He drove well below the speed limit (35-40 mph in a 50 mph zone) due to fog, showing prudence.

He checked his side mirrors as he slowed.

He kept his foot on the brake, ensuring bright brake lights were continuously visible to approaching traffic.

Counter Argument (Panko): Panko will argue stopping in the lane was reckless.

Rebuttal (Dahir): Given the lack of a shoulder and the immediate emergency (Tram was "dazed"), stopping to assess for 15-30 seconds while using brake lights is, at worst, mere negligence (failure to perfectly meet the duty), which is protected by the GSA (Miller).

IV. Conclusion for Summary Judgment

MSJ Rationale: Since Dahir provided direct evidence of his intent to render aid (meeting the GSA standard) and his actions demonstrate caution rather than reckless disregard (avoiding the gross negligence exception), there is no genuine issue of material fact regarding his GSA immunity. Judgment must be granted.

III. Comprehensive Guide for the Performance Test, February 2024

Initial Read Through

The primary goal of the initial read is to determine the standard of review and the winning legal hook before diving deep into the facts.

Read the Task Memo FIRST:

The memo requires a Memorandum of Points and Authorities supporting a Motion for Summary Judgment (MSJ). This immediately sets the extremely high standard: proving there is no triable issue of material fact and the Defendant is entitled to Judgment as a Matter of Law (JML). The entire case rests on the Columbia Good Samaritan Act (GSA) (CS 34-30).

Read the Law Library (Statute and Cases):

GSA (CS 34-30): Establish the two core requirements for immunity: good faith and gratuitously renders emergency care, noting the single exception is gross negligence.

Chung v. Delva: This case is the blueprint and the obstacle. It confirms that stopping and inquiring can be "rendering emergency care." Crucially, it reversed summary judgment because the defendant failed to provide direct evidence of their own subjective intent to aid. STRATEGY: The facts in our case (Panko v. Dahir) must be used to distinguish Chung by providing this exact missing evidence.

Miller v. Jones: Defines the high bar for the exception. Gross Negligence requires a reckless disregard of a legal duty, showing utter unconcern. Simple failure to adequately meet a duty is only mere negligence, which is protected by GSA.

Read the Fact File (Seeking Specific Evidence):

Highlight the specific facts that prove Dahir's subjective intent (to distinguish Chung) and Dahir's REGARD for safety (to defeat the Miller standard).

Precise Issue Spotting

The entire MSJ argument must be based on a clear, two part legal syllogism demonstrating that the facts allow for only one conclusion: Dahir is immune.

GSA Application: Proving "Emergency Care" (The Intent Requirement):

The issue is whether John Dahir's act of stopping and talking to Tram constitutes "rendering emergency care" under the GSA.

The Winning Argument: Dahir provided direct evidence of his subjective intent to render aid (he thought Tram was "possibly injured," asked "Are you okay?", and offered 911). This is the factual distinction that overcomes Chung and establishes immunity as a matter of law.

GSA Exception: Disproving "Gross Negligence" (The Conduct Requirement):

The issue is whether Dahir's conduct (stopping his semi in the roadway) constitutes gross negligence that would strip his immunity.

The Winning Argument: Dahir's actions show REGARD for safety, not "reckless disregard." He drove slow, activated his brake lights, and acted quickly in an immediate emergency. Therefore, his conduct was, at worst, mere negligence, which the GSA protects under Miller v. Jones.

Key Facts

These are the non disputed facts that must be leveraged in the analysis to prove that only a single legal inference, immunity, is possible.

Dahir's Direct Intent: Dahir's deposition stating he stopped because he thought Tram was "possibly injured" is the most powerful fact. This directly addresses and cures the deficiency noted by the Supreme Court in Chung.

Safety Measures (Brake Lights): Dahir confirms the semi's brake lights were on, and witness Higgins confirmed seeing them. This proves a conscious, affirmative effort to warn approaching vehicles, which destroys any claim of "reckless disregard" for safety required for gross negligence.

Emergency Duration: The entire stop to collision sequence lasted only 15 to 30 seconds. This supports the decision to stop immediately to assess the emergency, given the lack of a suitable shoulder.

Panko's Own Negligence: Panko admitted he did not have time to brake due to poor visibility. While not part of the GSA defense, this reinforces that Panko's own negligent driving was the primary cause of the collision, minimizing the legal impact of Dahir's minimal negligence.

Structuring the Answer

The output must be a formal legal argument formatted as a Memorandum of Points and Authorities, omitting the Introduction, Facts, and Conclusion sections per the Task Memo.

I. THE DEFENDANT IS IMMUNE UNDER THE COLUMBIA GOOD SAMARITAN ACT. (Main Argument Heading)

A. John Dahir Rendered Emergency Care by Stopping to Assess an Apparent Emergency. (Focus on the GSA application and subjective intent; use Chung as the rule, then distinguish it with Dahir's facts).

B. Dahir's Actions Do Not Amount to Gross Negligence. (Focus on avoiding the GSA exception; use Miller to define the rule, then apply facts of caution to prove mere negligence).

Step by Step Process

State the MSJ Standard: Begin the Argument section by stating the standard for a Motion for Summary Judgment, that the undisputed facts show the moving party is entitled to judgment as a matter of law.

Argue GSA Application: Under Section I.A, immediately prove Dahir qualifies for immunity by:

Stating the GSA rule (CS 34-30) and the Chung principle that assessing an accident is "emergency care."

Applying Dahir's direct testimony (thought Tram was injured, asked if he was okay) to establish subjective good faith intent as a matter of law, thereby distinguishing the facts of Chung.

Argue Lack of Gross Negligence: Transition to Section I.B to defeat the exception:

State the Miller high standard for Gross Negligence ("reckless disregard," "utter unconcern").

Apply facts of caution (slow speed, brake lights, short duration) to prove Dahir acted with REGARD for safety, demonstrating his conduct was, at worst, mere negligence, which is protected by the GSA.

Conclude: Provide a strong concluding sentence for the entire argument section, reiterating that the undisputed material facts preclude a finding of gross negligence and demonstrate immunity, thereby requiring a grant of summary judgment.

IV. Ultra Concise Answer, Performance Test, February 2024

MEMORANDUM OF POINTS AND AUTHORITIES

The Defendant, John Dahir, is entitled to Summary Judgment because the undisputed material facts establish immunity under the Columbia Good Samaritan Act (GSA) as a matter of law. Summary judgment is appropriate where there is no genuine issue of material fact and the moving party is entitled to judgment as a matter of law.

I. THE DEFENDANT IS IMMUNE UNDER THE COLUMBIA GOOD SAMARITAN ACT.

A. John Dahir Rendered Emergency Care by Stopping to Assess an Apparent Emergency.

The GSA provides immunity for a person who, in good faith, gratuitously renders emergency care at the scene of an accident (CS §34−30). The Columbia Supreme Court holds that merely stopping at an accident scene to assess the situation and inquire whether assistance is needed constitutes "rendering aid" under the GSA (Chung v. Delva).

The undisputed facts demonstrate Dahir's subjective good faith intent, which was absent in Chung. Dahir testified that he stopped because he saw a "heavily damaged" van and thought Mr. Tram was "possibly injured," immediately asking, "Are you okay?" **This direct evidence of intent establishes, as a matter of law, that Dahir was rendering emergency care and qualifies for GSA immunity.**

B. Dahir's Actions Do Not Amount to Gross Negligence.

GSA immunity can only be lost through gross negligence (CS §34−30). Gross negligence requires a conscious, voluntary act in reckless disregard of a legal duty or with utter unconcern for the safety of others (Miller v. Jones). Conduct that merely fails to adequately meet a duty is only mere negligence, which the GSA protects (Miller).

Dahir's actions do not meet this high bar. The undisputed facts show Dahir maintained a REGARD for safety: he drove slow (35-40 mph in heavy fog), confirmed his brake lights were on (verified by Higgins), and acted quickly (stop to collision took only 15–30 seconds). This conduct demonstrates, at worst, mere negligence in lane placement, but not the reckless disregard required by Miller. **Because the facts preclude a finding of gross negligence, Dahir is entitled to judgment as a matter of law.**

July 2023

California
Bar
Examination

Performance Test
INSTRUCTIONS AND FILE

IN RE MARRIAGE OF BURKE

Instructions ....

FILE

Memorandum to Applicant from Andrew Washington ....

Reporter's Transcript of Proceedings ....

The Washington Law Group

7 Chadbourn Road

Fair Haven, Columbia

MEMORANDUM

TO: Applicant
FROM: Andrew Washington
DATE: July 25, 2023
RE: In re Marriage of Burke

We represent Wendy Burke in this proceeding for dissolution of her marriage to Harlan Burke.

On July 21, 2023, the family court conducted a trial on the issue of the characterization of shares in the stock of DigitalAudio, Inc. that had been issued to Harlan before marriage. During marriage, the value of Harlan's DigitalAudio shares increased by $200 million. If the court were to characterize the increase entirely as community property, Wendy would effectively receive 50 percent or $100 million, with Harlan receiving the remaining $100 million. But if the court were to characterize the increase entirely as Harlan's separate property, Wendy would effectively receive nothing, with Harlan receiving the entire $200 million. The court has scheduled argument for July 26, 2023.

This morning, Harlan's counsel called me and offered to enter into a joint stipulation characterizing the increase in value, during marriage, of Harlan's DigitalAudio shares as 50 percent community property and 50 percent Harlan's separate property, a characterization that would effectively result in Wendy receiving $50 million and Harlan receiving $150 million. I called Wendy and relayed the offer to her. She asked me whether I would recommend that she accept Harlan's counsel's offer.

Please draft a letter to Wendy, for my signature, responding to her request. Begin with a brief statement of your recommendation, then address and resolve the following issues raised by her request, citing the applicable law and the material facts:

1. Are Harlan's DigitalAudio shares community property or separate property?

2. Did the community devote more than minimal effort involving Harlan's DigitalAudio shares during marriage so as to acquire an interest in any increase in value, during marriage, of the shares resulting in community property?

3. How should the family court apportion the $200 million increase in value, during marriage, of Harlan's DigitalAudio shares?

REPORTER'S TRANSCRIPT OF PROCEEDINGS

TRIAL ON ISSUE OF CHARACTERIZATION OF PROPERTY

July 21, 2023

9:00 a.m.

Family Court of Columbia, County of Dixon

In re Marriage of Burke, Case No. 123632

Maryann Moreno, Judge Presiding

THE CLERK: Please remain seated and come to order. The Family Court is now in session, the Honorable Maryann Moreno, judge presiding.

Your Honor, this is the matter of *In re Marriage of Burke*, and it's case number 123632. Counsel, may I have your appearances for the record?

MR. WASHINGTON: Good morning, Your Honor. Andrew Washington for Petitioner Wendy Burke, who is present.

THE COURT: Good morning, Mr. Washington.

MS. GRANADOS: Good morning, Your Honor. Karina Granados for Respondent Harlan Burke, who is also present.

THE COURT: Good morning, Ms. Granados.

We're here today for trial on the issue of the characterization of shares of stock in DigitalAudio, Inc., issued to Mr. Burke before marriage. This matter was originally assigned to Judge Sean Onderick when Ms. Burke filed the petition for dissolution in 2021. On Judge Onderick's recent retirement, it was reassigned to me. Mr. Washington, call your first witness.

MR. WASHINGTON: Your Honor, before calling our first witness, I would like to read into the record a joint stipulation of facts between Ms. Burke and Mr. Burke.

THE COURT: Ms. Granados, there's a joint stipulation?

MS. GRANADOS: Yes, Your Honor.

THE COURT: Proceed then, Mr. Washington.

MR. WASHINGTON: Thank you, Your Honor.

Petitioner Wendy Burke and Respondent Harlan Burke jointly stipulate as follows:

1. In 1983, Harlan Burke co-founded DigitalAudio, Inc., with Pamela Gardner.
2. In founding DigitalAudio, Harlan Burke and Pamela Gardner each made a capital contribution of $5,000, and each received 50 percent of the shares of its stock.
3. In 1989, Harlan Burke and Wendy Burke married. By the date of marriage, the value of Harlan Burke's DigitalAudio shares had fallen to zero.
4. In 2009, Harlan Burke and Wendy Burke separated. By the date of separation, the value of Harlan Burke's DigitalAudio shares had risen to $200 million.

THE COURT: Ms. Granados, is this your joint stipulation?

MS. GRANADOS: Yes it is, Your Honor.

THE COURT: Just one question, Mr. Washington, solely out of curiosity. Ms. Burke and Mr. Burke separated in 2009. But it was not until 2021 that Ms. Burke filed the underlying petition. Why so long?

MR. WASHINGTON: Ms. Burke had raised four children with Mr. Burke, relatively amicably, and had not contemplated remarriage. In 2021, she began to contemplate remarriage.

THE COURT: Thank you, Mr. Washington. Call your first witness.

MR. WASHINGTON: Thank you, Your Honor. We call Petitioner Wendy Burke to the stand.

WENDY BURKE,

called as a witness for Petitioner Wendy Burke, having been duly sworn, testified as follows:

DIRECT EXAMINATION

MR. WASHINGTON: Q. Good morning, Ms. Burke.

A. Good morning.

Q. When did you meet Mr. Burke?

A. In 1986.

Q. How?

A. Through Pam — Pamela Gardner. She was a high school friend, and thought I'd like Harlan.

Q. Did you?

A. Yes, very much. He was so different from me, but in a good way. He had just graduated from the University of Columbia with a degree in computer science and electrical engineering; I was about to graduate with a degree in Classics – that's Latin and Greek.

Q. Was Mr. Burke working at DigitalAudio in 1986?

A. Yes, night and day. Typical start-up.

Q. When did you marry?

A. 1989.

Q. When did you separate?

A. 2009.

Q. Did Mr. Burke work at DigitalAudio throughout that time?

A. Yes. Night and day.

Q. Did you ever work at DigitalAudio?

A. Maybe not *at* DigitalAudio, but *for* DigitalAudio. In the early days of our marriage, I helped Harlan with shipping some hardware and software.

Q. Did you ever work outside the home?

A. Not *outside* the home, but *in* the home, just as hard as Harlan worked at DigitalAudio. Over the years, we had four children. I worked more than full time caring for them, for Harlan, and for the house.

Q. Do you work outside the home now?

A. At my age, and with a degree in Classics, no.

Q. Are you getting by?

A. Barely.

MR. WASHINGTON: Thank you, Ms. Burke. That's all I have.

THE COURT: Cross-examination, Ms. Granados?

MS. GRANADOS: Yes, Your Honor.

CROSS-EXAMINATION

MS. GRANADOS: Q. Good morning, Ms. Burke.

A. Good morning.

Q. You just testified that "I worked more than full time caring for them"—your four children—"for Harlan, and for the house."

A. Yes.

Q. But isn't it true that you didn't *have* to "work more than full time"?

A. No.

Q. But isn't it true that, many times over the years, Mr. Burke offered to hire housekeepers, nannies, drivers, and whatever other household staff you might have needed to enable you to pursue any career you wished, but that you refused?

A. Yes.

Q. Why?

A. I just preferred to raise my own children myself, especially with Harlan working night and day at DigitalAudio.

MS. GRANADOS: Thank you, Ms. Burke. That's all.

THE COURT: Redirect, Mr. Washington?

MR. WASHINGTON: No, Your Honor.

THE COURT: Call your next witness.

MR. WASHINGTON: We have none, Your Honor. Ms. Burke rests.

THE COURT: Ms. Granados, do you have any witnesses?

MS. GRANADOS: Yes, Your Honor. Mr. Burke.

HARLAN BURKE,

called as a witness for Respondent Harlan Burke, having been duly sworn, testified as follows:

DIRECT EXAMINATION

MS. GRANADOS: Q. Good morning, Mr. Burke.

A. Good morning.

Q. Did Ms. Burke ever do any work at or for DigitalAudio.

A. No.

Q. Did you ever offer to hire household staff to enable Ms. Burke to pursue a career?

A. Yes, many times.

Q. Did she ever take you up on any of your offers?

A. No.

MS. GRANADOS: Thank you, Mr. Burke. That's all.

THE COURT: Cross-examination, Mr. Washington?

MR. WASHINGTON: Yes, Your Honor.

CROSS-EXAMINATION

MR. WASHINGTON: Q. Good morning, Mr. Burke.

A. Good morning.

Q. Isn't it true that, over the years, you've often said that Ms. Burke was a great wife and mother?

A. Yes—and I meant it.

Q. You just heard Ms. Burke testify that she is "barely getting by," didn't you?

A. Yes.

Q. Isn't it true that you're "getting by" quite well?

A. Yes, very comfortably. I can't complain.

MR. WASHINGTON: Thank you, Mr. Burke. That's all I have.

THE COURT: Redirect, Ms. Granados?

MS. GRANADOS: No, Your Honor.

THE COURT: Ms. Granados, do you have any further witnesses?

MS. GRANADOS: Yes, Your Honor. One more, Pamela Gardner.

PAMELA GARDNER,
called as a witness for Respondent Harlan Burke, having been duly sworn,
testified as follows:

DIRECT EXAMINATION

MS. GRANADOS: Q. Good morning, Ms. Gardner.

A. Good morning.

Q. When did you meet Mr. Burke?

A. In 1981, when a bunch of us got together to form a band.

Q. Did you found DigitalAudio with Mr. Burke?

A. Yes.

Q. Why?

A. To transform the music recording industry by creating a market for cost-effective, privately-owned studios as an alternative to expensive commercial ones.

Q. What were your roles at DigitalAudio?

A. I was the Chief Executive Officer and Harlan was the Chief Scientific Officer.

Q. Was DigitalAudio able to transform the music recording industry?

A. Yes, I'm proud to say twice, through two entirely different products. Early on, there was SoundAudio, with its hardware and software. And later, there was ProAudio, with its entirely different hardware and software.

Q. Let me ask you about SoundAudio first. Who worked on it?

A. Harlan. He designed SoundAudio, updated SoundAudio, and sustained SoundAudio throughout its life as a marketable product.

Q. Did anyone work with Mr. Burke on SoundAudio?

A. No. SoundAudio was Harlan's baby. We were lucky Harlan stayed with DigitalAudio throughout its marketable life. No one else knew much about it.

Q. Did Mr. Burke also work on ProAudio later on?

A. No. Not at all. Others at DigitalAudio developed, updated, and sustained ProAudio.

Q. Did ProAudio derive from SoundAudio?

A. No, it was entirely different, both in hardware and software.

Q. In 2009, when, according to the joint stipulation, the value of Mr. Burke's DigitalAudio shares was $200 million, was SoundAudio a marketable product?

A. No, SoundAudio had ended its marketable life years earlier in 2009.

Q. In 2009, was ProAudio a marketable product?

A. Yes.

Q. In your opinion as DigitalAudio's Chief Executive Officer, what was the basis of the value of DigitalAudio's shares in 2009—SoundAudio or ProAudio?

MR. WASHINGTON: Objection: Impermissible opinion.

THE COURT: Overruled. A businessperson like Ms. Gardner may present an opinion based on her knowledge and participation in the day-to-day affairs of the business. [To the witness:] You may answer.

THE WITNESS: ProAudio.

MS. GRANADOS: Thank you, Ms. Gardner. That's all.

THE COURT: Cross-examination, Mr. Washington?

MR. WASHINGTON: Yes, Your Honor.

CROSS-EXAMINATION

MR. WASHINGTON: Q. Good morning, Ms. Gardner.

A. Good morning.

Q. Between 1989, the date of marriage, and 2009, the date of separation, was Mr. Burke important to DigitalAudio?

A. Yes, indeed. Without Harlan, DigitalAudio would not have come into existence and would not have remained in existence. He was always working, always at 110 percent. He's one of the most skilled computer scientists and electrical engineers of his generation, and he attracted many other skilled computer scientists and electrical engineers to DigitalAudio.

Q. But how could Mr. Burke be important to DigitalAudio if he had nothing to do with ProAudio?

A. ProAudio got off to a very rocky start. After initial development, it had to be redeveloped, not once, but several times. Harlan was able to keep updating SoundAudio, and DigitalAudio was able to keep selling SoundAudio, until ProAudio became marketable. Without Harlan, DigitalAudio would have gone out of business and it would never have developed ProAudio.

MR. WASHINGTON: Thank you, Ms. Gardner. That's all I have.

THE COURT: Redirect, Ms. Granados?

MS. GRANADOS: No, Your Honor. Mr. Burke rests.

THE COURT: We've come to the end of presentation of evidence and all that remains is argument. I've got another matter I have to handle this afternoon. Let's reconvene for argument at the same time in five days, if that fits your schedules.

MR. WASHINGTON: That's fine with me, Your Honor.

MS. GRANADOS: It's fine with me as well.

THE COURT: Excellent. See you then.

July 2023

California
Bar
Examination

Performance Test
LIBRARY

IN RE MARRIAGE OF BURKE

LIBRARY

In re Marriage of Rand
Columbia Court of Appeal (2015)..

In re Marriage of Rand

Columbia Court of Appeal (2015)

In this proceeding for dissolution of marriage, Linda Rand appeals from an order characterizing shares of stock in Rand Investment Corporation (RIC), which Charles Rand formed before marriage. Finding no error in the order, we shall affirm.

FACTUAL BACKGROUND AND PROCEDURAL HISTORY

In 1974, Charles formed RIC to provide investment advisory services in exchange for fees based on the percentage of clients' assets under management. Charles owned all of RIC's shares and would continue to do so over the following years.

In 1986, Charles married Linda. As of the date of marriage, the value of Charles's RIC shares was zero.

Between 1986 and 1991, Charles worked for RIC night and day; Linda was not involved with the business at all. The value of Charles's RIC shares rose from zero to the tens of millions of dollars.

Between 1991 and 2004, lifted by an ever-rising market, RIC became enormously successful. By 1991, Charles had withdrawn from the business, having left it essentially on autopilot, and had turned from making money to spending money. Linda remained uninvolved with the business. The value of Charles's RIC shares rose from the tens of millions of dollars to the hundreds of millions. Charles and Linda amassed $300 million in cash.

In 2004, Charles and Linda separated. As of the date of separation, the value of Charles's RIC shares, as noted, had risen to the hundreds of millions of dollars.

In 2005, Charles filed a petition for dissolution of marriage. Charles and Linda soon entered into a joint stipulation distributing all of their $300 million in cash, giving each $150 million.

In 2011, after extensive—and to our mind, excessive—discovery and motion practice by Charles and Linda, the family court conducted a trial on the issue of the characterization of Charles's RIC shares.

In 2012, the family court issued an order with a statement of decision. The court: (1) characterized Charles's RIC shares as his separate property; (2) characterized, as community property, the increase in the value of his shares between the date of the marriage in 1986 and his withdrawal from the business in 1991, under *Pereira v. Pereira* (Colum. Supreme Ct., 1909); and (3) characterized, as Charles's separate property, the increase in the value of his shares between his withdrawal from the business in 1991 and the date of separation in 2004, under *Van Camp v. Van Camp* (Colum. Ct. App., 1921). The court awarded Linda tens of millions of dollars consisting of her 50 percent share of the community property, and awarded Charles hundreds of millions of dollars consisting of: (1) his 50 percent share of the community property; and (2) his 100 percent of his separate property. It is from this order that Linda has appealed.

DISCUSSION

Under Columbia law, marriage is an egalitarian partnership.

Property that either spouse acquires during marriage belongs to the marital community—it is community property. *See*, Columbia Family Code, section 760. At dissolution, community property is awarded to each spouse in an equal 50 percent share. *Id.* Section 2550.

In contrast, property that either spouse acquired before marriage belongs to that spouse—it is his or her separate property. *See id.* Section 770. Likewise, the proceeds of property that either spouse acquired before marriage also belong to that spouse—the proceeds are also his or her separate property—even if he or she acquires the proceeds during marriage. *See id.* At dissolution, separate property is confirmed in its entirety to the owning spouse. *Id.* Section 2550.

But because marriage is an egalitarian partnership, whenever the community devotes more than minimal effort involving a spouse's separate property during marriage, the community acquires an interest in any increase in value, during marriage, of the separate property, and that interest is community property. *In re Marriage of Dekker* (Colum. Ct. App., 1993).

It follows that, in dividing property at dissolution, the family court must apportion the increase in value, during marriage, of one spouse's separate property whenever the community devotes more than minimal effort involving the separate property during marriage.

One approach to apportionment, under *Pereira*, applies when the increase in value, during marriage, of one spouse's separate property is principally due to community efforts—i.e., when such efforts are the predominant cause of the increase. This approach requires the family court to apportion the increase in value mainly to the community estate (with the remainder to the owning spouse's separate estate).

Another approach to apportionment, under *Van Camp*, applies when the increase in value, during marriage, of one spouse's separate property is principally due to factors *other than* community efforts—again, when such efforts are the predominant cause of the increase. This approach requires the family court to apportion the increase in value mainly to the estate of the owning spouse (with the remainder to the community estate).

Finally, although in dividing property at dissolution the family court is not required to adopt either the *Pereira* approach or the *Van Camp* approach—or indeed any other approach—the court must nevertheless divide the property in such a way as to achieve substantial justice between the spouses.

After review, we conclude that the family court properly characterized Charles's RIC shares as his separate property. It is undisputed that Charles acquired his shares before marriage.

We also conclude that the family court properly determined that the community acquired an interest in the increase in value, during marriage, of Charles's RIC shares. It is similarly undisputed that the community devoted more than minimal effort involving Charles's shares during marriage through Charles's hard work for the business between marriage in 1986 and separation in 1991. Although there is no evidence that Linda worked for the business, that fact is inconsequential. The community acts whenever either of the spouses acts.

Against this background, Linda contends that the family court erred by adopting a "hybrid *Pereira/Van Camp* approach." We disagree. The facts show two separate periods during marriage: The first period, between 1986 and 1991, was the "*Pereira* period," during which the increase in value of Charles's RIC shares was principally due to community efforts, i.e., Charles's hard work was the predominant cause of the increase. The second period, between 1991 and 2004, was the "*Van Camp* period," during which the increase in value of Charles's RIC shares was principally due to factors *other than* community efforts, i.e., market forces were the predominant cause of the increase.

Linda goes on to contend that the family court erroneously subjected her to substantial injustice by awarding Charles hundreds of millions of dollars and awarding her *only* tens of millions. The court, of course, did not leave Linda destitute. Even if it had, it would not have mattered. Contrary to Linda's assumption, substantial justice between the spouses does *not* require the court to evenly divide the *entire* increase in value, during marriage, of one spouse's separate property. Instead, it requires the court to evenly divide only the *portion* of the increase *principally due to community efforts*. That is what the court did.

DISPOSITION

For the reasons stated, the order of the family court is AFFIRMED.

July 2023 California General Bar Examination Performance Test

PERFORMANCE TEST

II. Concise Outline for the Performance Test, July 2023

The required task is to draft a Letter to the Client (Wendy Burke) recommending whether to accept a settlement offer regarding the characterization and apportionment of Separate Property (SP) stock appreciation that occurred during the marriage.

Characterization of DigitalAudio Shares (Issue 1)

Rule: Property acquired before marriage is Separate Property (SP). (Columbia Family Code § 770; In re Marriage of Rand).

Fact: Harlan co-founded the company in 1983, before the 1989 marriage.

Critical Fact: The stipulated value of Harlan's shares had fallen to zero by the date of marriage (1989).

Conclusion: The shares are initially Harlan's SP, but the initial SP capital is effectively zero for the purpose of apportionment calculations.

Community Effort & Acquisition of Interest (Issue 2)

Rule: The community acquires an apportionable interest in SP appreciation if community labor contributed more than minimal effort involving the separate property during marriage. (In re Marriage of Dekker, cited in Rand).

Fact: Harlan worked full-time, "night and day," as the Chief Scientific Officer (CSO) throughout the marriage (1989-2009).

Fact: Co-founder testified that Harlan's work was essential to keep the company solvent (SoundAudio) until the profitable product (ProAudio) became marketable.

Conclusion: Harlan's full-time effort was unequivocally more than minimal and was the essential causal factor in the company's survival, making the increase subject to apportionment.

Apportionment of Value Increase (Pereira vs. Van Camp) (Issue 3)

Rule: The court applies the formula based on the predominant cause of the increase in value during marriage (In re Marriage of Rand).

Pereira: Applies when the increase is principally due to community efforts (personal skill/talent). Value is mainly apportioned to CP.

Van Camp: Applies when the increase is principally due to factors other than community efforts (inherent nature/market forces). Value is mainly apportioned to SP.

Argument (Favors Community): The Pereira Formula is mandated. Harlan's personal skill as a CSO and his effort in sustaining the company's existence was the predominant cause of the $200 million appreciation.

Pereira Calculation: SP receives a fixed, fair rate of return (e.g., 10%) on the initial capital. Since the initial capital value was zero at marriage, the SP return is also zero. The entire remainder (nearly 100%) of the $200 million appreciation is Community Property (CP).

Recommendation: The court will likely award the community the vast majority of the $200 million increase ($100 million to Wendy). The settlement offer of $50 million (25% CP) is grossly inadequate.

III. Comprehensive Guide for the Performance Test, July 2023

This Performance Test requires the application of Community Property principles for the apportionment of separate property that appreciates during marriage due to the managing spouse's labor. The goal is to draft a clear Letter to the Client (Wendy Burke) leading to the recommendation to REJECT the settlement offer.

Initial Read Through

Document Type and Tone: Draft a professional yet clear Letter to the Client. The tone should be objective in the legal analysis but advisory in the conclusion.

The Legal Framework: The case of In re Marriage of Rand provides the exact rules, definitions, and application framework necessary, focusing on the "predominant cause" test.

The Factual and Legal Hammer: The two most critical facts are:

1) Harlan's shares were valued at $0 at the date of marriage, and

2) Harlan's work was deemed essential for the company's survival (Co-founder testimony).

These facts combine to overwhelmingly mandate the Pereira Formula and result in a near total award of the appreciation to the Community.

Precise Issue Spotting

Issue 1 & 2 (Threshold): Determine the initial characterization (SP) and establish that the full-time, "night and day" labor by Harlan was "more than minimal effort" (Rand citing Dekker), thereby subjecting the appreciation to apportionment.

Issue 3 (The Decisive Issue): The key is proving that Harlan's personal skill and effort was the predominant cause of the appreciation, not market forces. The co-founder's testimony that the company would have gone out of business without Harlan's continued work is the direct link that triggers the Pereira Formula (appreciation due to community effort).

Key Facts

Initial Value: $0 at marriage in 1989.

Appreciation: $200 million by separation in 2009.

Harlan's Role: Chief Scientific Officer, working "night and day."

Causation: Co-founder stated Harlan's work on SoundAudio prevented the company from going out of business, which was necessary for ProAudio to be developed. This establishes Harlan's skill as the predominant cause of the entity's survival and subsequent growth.

Wendy's Contribution: Stayed home to raise children, supporting Harlan's full-time work, which provides a strong equitable basis for the community's claim.

Structuring the Answer (Letter to Client)

The letter must follow the Task Memo's required structure:

Recommendation (First Sentence): State the recommendation to REJECT the offer.

Issue 1: Discuss initial characterization and the $0 starting value.

Issue 2: Discuss more than minimal effort based on Harlan's CSO role and necessity.

Issue 3 (Detailed Discussion): Argue forcefully for Pereira based on the "predominant cause" test from Rand. Explain the financial mechanics: SP return on $0 capital is $0, meaning the entire $200 million residual goes to the CP.

Step by Step Process

Draft Header and Recommendation: Start immediately with the formal Memorandum header and the clear, first-sentence recommendation to REJECT.

Analyze Issues 1 & 2: Use the stipulated facts to state the initial SP characterization and the "more than minimal effort" conclusion, citing the CSO role and the necessity of his work. Cite Columbia Family Code § 770 and In re Marriage of Dekker.

Analyze Issue 3: State the Pereira rule from Rand and apply it directly, using the co-founder's testimony to satisfy the "predominant cause" requirement. Detail the financial calculation, emphasizing that a return on zero capital yields zero for the Separate Property, thereby characterizing the entire $200 million appreciation as Community Property.

Final Polish: Ensure the word count is within the 250-325 limit, and the tone is professional and advisory.

IV. Ultra Concise Answer, Performance Test, July 2023

MEMORANDUM

TO: Wendy Burke
FROM: Andrew Washington
DATE: July 25, 2023
RE: In re Marriage of Burke, Recommendation on DigitalAudio Stock

Dear Wendy:

I recommend you **REJECT** Harlan's 50/50 settlement offer. Our legal position is exceptionally strong because the original stock value at marriage was zero, and the appreciation is due to Harlan's personal efforts, mandating the application of the Pereira Formula.

1. Characterization of DigitalAudio Shares.

The shares Harlan acquired pre-marriage are his Separate Property (SP) (Colum. Fam. Code § 770). However, the stipulated value of the shares had fallen to zero by the date of marriage (1989).

2. Community Effort and Interest in Value Increase.

The community devoted more than minimal effort to DigitalAudio (In re Marriage of Dekker). Harlan worked full-time as the Chief Scientific Officer (CSO) throughout the 1989–2009 marriage. His co-founder confirmed his continuous work on SoundAudio was essential to keep the company solvent until the profitable ProAudio product became marketable. This full-time community labor grants the community an interest in the $200 million appreciation.

3. Apportionment of the $200 Million Increase.

The court must apportion the increase based on the predominant cause (In re Marriage of Rand). We argue for the Pereira Formula, as Harlan's personal skill was the predominant cause of the company's survival and thus its ability to appreciate. Under Pereira, Harlan's SP receives only a fixed return on the initial capital. Since the SP capital value was zero, the SP's return is also zero.

The entire residual $200 million must therefore be characterized as Community Property (CP), entitling you to $100 million. The offer of $50 million is inadequate.

Sincerely,

Andrew Washington

February 2023

California
Bar
Examination

Performance Test

INSTRUCTIONS AND FILE

STATE v. HUGHES

Instructions ....

FILE

Memorandum to Applicant from Jan Dauss ....

Transcript of Pretrial Hearing ....

Transcript of Interview of Sebastian Hughes ....

OFFICE OF THE STATE ATTORNEY
County of Gaston
Littleton, Columbia

MEMORANDUM

TO: Applicant

FROM: Jan Dauss, State's Attorney

DATE: February 21, 2023

RE: State v. Hughes

Defendant, Sebastian Hughes, is charged with murder after he fatally stabbed his uncle, Peter Gault, during a dispute over a Corvette car engine. Defendant asserts he acted in self-defense. A centerpiece of our case against Defendant is a recorded statement Defendant made to detectives while he was in the hospital recovering from a stab wound inflicted by his uncle.

Defendant originally moved to suppress the statement based on a failure to be given *Miranda* warnings. The judge ruled in the State's favor on that motion. Defendant now argues that the statement was not voluntary and therefore should be excluded from his trial. The court decided that this new motion does not need to be briefed, but the court does want oral argument.

Please draft the oral argument I will give in opposition to suppression of the statement. Our success depends on our ability to marshal the facts. Do not start with a statement of facts as you would if you were writing a brief. Rather, weave the specific facts into your argument as they relate to each of the elements of the controlling law.

Attached are the transcript of the recorded statement and a portion of the transcript where the court refused to suppress the statement on *Miranda* grounds. While you are not to address the *Miranda* issue, the court's characterization of the interview may be helpful to your argument.

State v. Hughes

Transcript of Pretrial Hearing

February 17, 2023

COURT: Let's first deal with defense counsel's motion to exclude Defendant's statement for failure to be given *Miranda* warnings. I have read counsels' briefs and listened to the recorded statement. I have decided that the circumstances in this case overwhelmingly demonstrate that Defendant was not in custody for *Miranda* purposes. The motion is denied.

Does Defendant plan any other motions?

DEFENSE COUNSEL: Your Honor, Defendant moves to exclude the statement made while confined in the hospital as involuntary. At the time of his questioning, Defendant was not sufficiently lucid and the coercive surrounding circumstances of the questioning were such that, under the United States Supreme Court's *Mincey v. Arizona*, his statement was not the result of a rational intellect and free will. Defendant was at the complete mercy of the detectives because he was in physical shock from being stabbed in the lung and in mental shock from being involved in the death of his uncle. I think everyone will agree that Defendant sustained a stab injury. He had to go through surgery in order to recover from that injury. He was administered pain medication. Further, he was still under the constant care of a medical professional while the interview began and as it progressed. I don't know exactly what the medication was at that point, but it was pain medication consistent with surgery.

COURT: Does the State stipulate to these facts?

DISTRICT ATTORNEY: We certainly do not stipulate to the allegations characterizing the lucidity of Defendant or the coercive nature of the questioning. It is also unclear what medication Defendant was on at that point. The rest of the facts we would concede.

COURT: All right. As I said, I have listened to the recording of the statement. I don't think I need briefs on this motion. The law is pretty straightforward. I would, however, like to hear counsels' arguments on the point. Let's schedule those arguments five days from today at 9:00 a.m. See you then counsel.

Transcript of Interview of Sebastian Hughes with Detectives Ray and Martindale August 22, 2022

DETECTIVE RAY: Good evening Mr. Hughes, I'm Detective Ray and this is .....

HUGHES: He's dead?

RAY: If you mean Peter Gault, yes, he's dead. Mr. Hughes, this is my partner, Detective Martindale. We need to ask you some questions about what happened. You understand you're not under arrest, right? You do? You're nodding yes. Are you able to speak?

HUGHES: I've got tubes in both my lungs and I'm a little drugged up, but yeah, I can speak. It's just, I can't believe it.

RAY: We need to interview you. Our job is to come in when someone passes away. We weren't there. We don't know what happened. If it's okay, we are going to tape record our interview.

HUGHES: It's okay.

RAY: We are starting the interview with Mr. Sebastian Hughes in the surgical observation unit of the hospital at 7:50 p.m., after calling the hospital about three or four times throughout the day to see if you were well enough to speak with us. We understand that you were injured around 11:30 this morning. You've been in the hospital about 8 hours. You got out of surgery two hours ago.

Just for our record, Mr. Hughes, I want to describe what I see. Mr. Hughes is shirtless and lying down kind of in a quasi-seated position with his back kind of at maybe a 45–degree angle in his bed in his room. Mr. Hughes has redness or an abrasion on his forehead, and a stab wound on his right side near the right chest area under the armpit.

Can you tell us what happened?

HUGHES: I've got to call my mom.

RAY: Mm–hm. What happened?

HUGHES: I received a phone call from my mom's brother, Peter Gault, this morning around 11:00 o'clock. He wanted to know the whereabouts of a Corvette engine he had been storing in the garage of my mom's house. I had sold the engine for $800 several months ago, and told him about the sale at that time. I reminded Peter that he had sold the engine to me and I figured it was mine to sell. He became angry.

RAY: Mm-hm.

HUGHES: I heard my mom crying in the background. I feared for her safety because Peter had a short temper and he was hot-headed when it came to her. I decided to leave work and drive to the house to make sure she was okay.

RAY: Did you go directly there?

HUGHES: I've really got to call my mom.

RAY: Yeah, yeah, will get to that. So, you were at work and decided to leave. What happened next?

HUGHES: I stopped at my work locker on my way out and placed an eight-inch wrench in my shirt pocket as protection, just in case it came to that.

UNIDENTIFIED VOICE: Excuse me officers, I'm from Cardiology and need to draw some blood from Mr. Hughes.

RAY: We'll get out of your way here.

HUGHES: You guys aren't leaving, are you?

RAY: No, we're not going anywhere. We will turn the tape off while medical staff draws blood and Detective Martindale and I stretch our legs.

BREAK IN RECORDING

RAY: Okay, we're back, Mr. Hughes. We left off just as you were going to the house. What happened when you got to the house?

HUGHES: Peter and my mom were standing in the driveway in front of his van. Peter was furious. My mom stood between Peter and me, crying her eyes out trying to keep us separate. She grabbed the wrench from my pocket. I guess to make sure I didn't use it on Peter.

We argued at first. Then things got wild. Eventually, Peter knocks me to the ground. He pushed my mom a couple of times and grabbed the wrench from my mom and tried to hit me with it. At some point, Peter either dropped the wrench or threw it at me. Somehow, it ended up on the ground.

RAY: So what happened then?

HUGHES: I bent down and tried to pick up the wrench. Peter said, "You're not gonna do anything with that," and kicked me real hard on the right side of my forehead. I wound up on the ground between the van and the truck. He had the wrench in his hand.

RAY: Mm-hm.

HUGHES: Peter ran to the back doors of his van. I thought he was going to grab a knife or tool from the van. So I pulled my knife from my boot. Peter saw me getting up with the knife and ran toward the front of the van and got his own knife. I chased him. He tripped and fell near the porch, but got up right away. He lunged at me, saying, "I'm gonna kill you," and that's when I stabbed him with my knife.

RAY: I'm sorry. I guess I missed where your knife comes into the story. Were you wearing the knife while at work?

HUGHES: Yeah, I guess I forgot to mention that I got it from my work locker when I got the wrench. I placed a big knife in my boot, underneath my pant leg. Because, you know, I know how he is.

I realized I had been stabbed only when I saw blood all over myself and could not breathe. I thought I was going to die and walked over to a neighboring house to lie in the shade.

RAY: Do you think that, if you didn't bring the knife, your uncle would be alive right now?

HUGHES: Probably, but I would still be in the hospital.

RAY: How do you know that?

HUGHES: I know. This was all self-defense, man. If I had not stabbed Peter, Peter would've killed me. You guys don't know what that man was capable of. Look, I see you're skeptical. You can give me a lie detector test, or check my phone records, or talk to my family to confirm the truth I'm telling you.

RAY: We may do that Mr. Hughes, but for now I think we have enough. You've been generous with your time and we need to let you rest.

HUGHES: I may stay awake. I'm going to try to watch the University of Columbia game on TV. I went there for a couple of years.

RAY: Enjoy. We'll be in touch.

Interview concluded at 8:20 p.m., August 22, 2022.

February 2023

California
Bar
Examination

Performance Test
LIBRARY

STATE v. HUGHES

<u>LIBRARY</u>

State v. Perdomo
Columbia Supreme Court (2007) ....

State v. Perdomo

Columbia Supreme Court (2007)

Defendant Gerson Perdomo was involved in a single-car accident in which he and another occupant of the car, Marco Quinonez, were seriously injured. A third occupant, Ismael Rodriguez, was killed. Defendant was convicted by a jury of felony vehicular manslaughter while driving intoxicated. The only seriously contested issue at trial was whether Defendant was the driver.

After a night of heavy drinking, at around 2:45 a.m. on August 23, 2003, Defendant was allegedly driving on the freeway at approximately 80 miles an hour when he crashed into, and nearly went over, the concrete center median. Rodriguez, found in the back seat, was pronounced dead when taken to a nearby hospital. Quinonez and Defendant were found in the front seat. Each had serious injuries.

Defendant based his defense on the contention that the other surviving occupant, Marco Quinonez, was driving at the time of the accident. Defendant moved pretrial to exclude the evidence of inculpatory statements he made to the police officers. Near the end of the interview, Defendant admitted he sometimes smoked marijuana and then said, "Maybe that day I was smoking. I'm not going to mess with you guys. I was driving Marco's car."

Defendant argued that admission of his statements violated his Fifth and Fourteenth Amendment rights to a fair trial. He claims it was error of constitutional dimension to admit statements he made to officers who interrogated him in the intensive care unit of the hospital while he was recovering from surgery and heavily sedated with narcotic pain medications.

Defendant suffered severe traumatic injuries to his chest area. Several of his ribs were fractured. He underwent emergency surgery to remove his spleen. He also had some bleeding in his brain.

Four days after the accident and Defendant's surgery, medical personnel in the intensive care unit of the hospital finally granted Officer Laubscher and his partner Officer Jensen permission to speak to Defendant. Medical personnel directed the officers to keep their discussion brief. Around 6:30 a.m., the officers interviewed Defendant in the intensive care unit of the hospital. The interview was tape recorded.

Defendant was lying flat on his bed, recovering from the splenectomy, broken ribs and head injury. He was in obvious pain. Defendant had received his last pain medication five and a half hours earlier. He was still connected to intravenous solutions and monitors. He had been on a ventilator since the surgery, but this device had been removed the day before and he was breathing on his own. Defendant's speech was slow and deliberate but not slurred or overly raspy from the intubation. The officers' questions were also slow, subdued and deliberate. The interview, with numerous pauses, lasted approximately 20 minutes.

The officers questioned Defendant about the events occurring before and after the accident. Defendant's answers were responsive to the officers' questions. Most significantly, according to Officer Jensen, who was present and later transcribed the tape, Defendant admitted he had been driving the car when the accident occurred.

A statement is involuntary if it is not the product of "a rational intellect and free will." *Mincey v. Arizona* (U.S. 1978). The question posed by the Due Process Clause in cases of claimed psychological coercion is whether the influences brought to bear upon the accused were such as to overbear petitioner's will to resist and bring about confessions not freely self-determined.

In determining whether or not an accused's will is overborne, an examination must be made of all the surrounding circumstances, including: 1) the characteristics of the accused, including such factors as the defendant's maturity, education, physical condition, and mental health (including mental acuity), and 2) the details of the interrogation that indicate coercion, which include the length of the interrogation, the location of the interrogation, and the interrogation's continuity. Additional factors that might indicate coercion include whether the officers dominated or controlled the course of the interrogation; whether they allowed defendant to tell his story, then asked follow-up questions to clarify the details; whether their questions were open-ended and neither aggressive nor particularly accusatory in nature; and whether there is evidence that the officers had or drew weapons or otherwise employed threatening or intimidating interrogation tactics. No single factor is dispositive.

Defendant asserts there are numerous parallels between his case and the factual circumstances of *Mincey v. Arizona*, sufficient to find his statements involuntary and require reversal of his convictions.

Surrounding Circumstances

1. Characteristics of the Accused

In *Mincey v. Arizona*, Mincey was shot in the hip by police officers in a raid on his apartment. Mincey was transported to the hospital where he received emergency treatment. When he arrived at the hospital, he was almost to the point of coma. The shot caused damage to the sciatic nerve and partial paralysis of his right leg. In the emergency room, tubes were inserted into his throat to help him breathe, and through his nose into his stomach to keep him from vomiting. A catheter was inserted into his bladder. He received various drugs, and medical personnel attached a device to his arm so he could be fed intravenously. Mincey was then moved from the emergency room into the intensive care unit.

Around 8:00 p.m., a police detective came to the intensive care unit to interrogate Mincey. The detective told Mincey he was under arrest for the murder of the police officer. He gave *Miranda* warnings to Mincey and then started questioning him about the activities and shooting at his apartment. Mincey could not talk because of the tube in his mouth. He responded to the detective's questions by writing answers on pieces of paper. The detective continued to question Mincey until almost midnight. During the interrogation, Mincey repeatedly asked for the interrogation to cease. Several times, Mincey requested the assistance of counsel before responding. He complained to the detective that the pain in his leg was unbearable. Some of Mincey's written responses were incoherent and on their face showed he was confused and unable to think clearly about the events at his apartment or about the interrogation.

The Supreme Court concluded Mincey's statements were not the product of his free and rational choice: "To the contrary, the undisputed evidence makes clear that Mincey wanted *not* to answer Detective Hust. But Mincey was weakened by pain and shock, isolated from family, friends, and legal counsel, and barely conscious, and his will was simply overborne. Due process of law requires that statements obtained as these were cannot be used in any way against a defendant at his trial."

Like the situation in *Mincey,* here Defendant was questioned while lying in a hospital bed in the intensive care unit. As in *Mincey,* no family members or friends were then with him. He was recovering from surgery for the injuries he received four days earlier. Intravenous tubes were still attached to his body. Defendant had been receiving narcotic pain medications since his admission to the hospital.

According to the interrogating officers, Defendant appeared to be in pain and also appeared to still be under the influence of the narcotic pain medication.

However, this is where the similarities end. Unlike what occurred in *Mincey,* Defendant was not interrogated within hours of his injuries, and not interrogated only a few hours after receiving medical treatment. Also unlike in *Mincey,* Defendant was not interrogated while going in and out of consciousness. In this case, the officers were not permitted to interview Defendant until four days after Defendant's surgery. Hospital personnel did not permit the officers to talk to Defendant until they determined he was "alert," "oriented," and could "obey commands," as indicated by his medical chart. By this time, Defendant no longer needed the assistance of a respirator and medical personnel had removed it the day before the interview.

On the day of the interview, hospital staff determined Defendant's condition had improved sufficiently so that he could safely be cared for in a regular hospital room. At 8:30 a.m., and two hours after the interview, Defendant was moved out of the intensive care unit, taken off intravenous pain medications and thereafter given oral doses of Vicodin for pain as needed.

The evidence showed Defendant was probably still under the influence of the pain medications, although the effect of the morphine he received five and a half hours earlier had likely diminished over the hours.

Nothing on the tape shows Defendant's thinking was impaired by the medications. Defendant's speech is slow and deliberate, but is not slurred or incoherent. Each of Defendant's answers is appropriate to the question asked. In some instances, his answers were detailed. For example, when asked the name of the security company for which they all worked, Defendant stated the name for the officers, spelled out the company name several times, and even recited the company's telephone number.

At the beginning of the tape it appears Defendant was even alert enough to attempt to deceive the officers. He initially told the officers the night of the accident that he had been driving his mother's Nissan, alone, and without passengers. He later acknowledged being with Rodriguez and Quinonez in Quinonez's mother's Honda.

2. *Details of the Interrogation*

In *Mincey*, the detective ceased the interrogation only during the intervals when Mincey lost consciousness or received medical treatment and after each such interruption returned relentlessly to his task. The statements at issue were thus the result of virtually continuous questioning of a seriously and painfully wounded man on the edge of consciousness.

Most importantly, the interrogation in the present case exhibits none of the coercive police activity found in *Mincey* and other cases finding statements to have been involuntary. The interview in the present case was relatively short. It lasted a maximum of 20 minutes, as compared to the three hours Mincey was forced to endure. The officers in the present case posed their questions in a calm, deliberate manner. The officers' voices on the tape are very quiet and subdued, perhaps in deference to the other patients in the unit, and/or because of the relative lack of privacy in the room. The 20-minute interview includes several pauses as well, as medical personnel enter and exit the room providing treatment for the other patients. Unlike Mincey, who had asked for the interrogation to cease and had refused to answer some questions without the assistance of counsel, Defendant made no such requests and did not express distress or otherwise indicate any unwillingness to speak to the officers.

As the trial court noted, the officers' tone was conversational and not threatening. One of the subjects discussed was how supportive and attentive Defendant's mother had been. Defendant expressed gratitude for his recovery. He asked the officers questions regarding his friends' conditions. At the end of the tape the officers wish Defendant good luck and a speedy recovery.

In short, the record is devoid of any suggestion the officers resorted to physical or psychological pressure to elicit statements from Defendant. Absent some indication of coercive police activity, an admission or confession cannot be deemed involuntary within the Due Process Clause of the Fourteenth Amendment.

The judgment is affirmed.

February 2023 California General Bar Examination Performance Test

II. Concise Outline for the Performance Test, February 2023

The required task is to draft an Objective Memorandum analyzing whether the defendant's statement to police while hospitalized should be excluded as involuntary under the Due Process Clause of the Fourteenth Amendment.

Admissibility of Hospital Confession (Due Process Involuntariness)

Rule: A statement is involuntary if it is not the product of a "rational intellect and free will," or if the influences brought to bear upon the accused were such as to overbear the petitioner's will to resist (State v. Perdomo citing Mincey v. Arizona).

Standard: The court examines the totality of the surrounding circumstances using a two-pronged test.

A. Characteristics of the Accused (Defendant's State)

Factors: Physical condition (injury, medication, pain), mental health, acuity, education, and maturity.

Argument for Involuntariness (Mincey parallels): Defendant was in the Intensive Care Unit, recovering from severe injury/surgery, attached to IVs/monitors, and administered narcotic pain medication.

Counter-Argument for Voluntariness (Perdomo distinction): Police were only allowed to speak to the defendant after medical personnel determined he was "alert, oriented, and could obey commands." The interview was conducted days (not hours) after the injury/surgery, and the defendant's answers must be examined for coherence, responsiveness, and detail.

B. Details of the Interrogation (Police Coercion)

Factors: Length, location, continuity, officers' tone, and presence of threats/intimidation. Crucially, there must be some indication of coercive police activity.

Argument for Involuntariness (Mincey parallels): Interrogation took place in the sensitive ICU, which is inherently isolating and coercive.

Counter-Argument for Voluntariness (Perdomo distinction): The interview was brief (e.g., 20 minutes max), the officers' questions were calm and subdued (not aggressive or accusatory), and the defendant did not ask for the interrogation to cease or request counsel. The record must be devoid of physical or psychological pressure.

III. Comprehensive Guide for the Performance Test, February 2023

This Performance Test requires you to write an Objective Memorandum analyzing the admissibility of a criminal defendant's statement made to police while the defendant was recovering in a hospital. The analysis centers entirely on the Due Process Clause (Fourteenth Amendment) and the concept of involuntary confessions.

Initial Read Through

Identify Document Type & Role: You are drafting an Objective Memorandum for a supervising attorney. Your role is to analyze, not advocate.

Identify the Core Issue: The central issue is the admissibility of the confession under the Due Process Clause (involuntariness) where the physical state of the defendant (injury, pain, medication) is the primary concern.

Map the Library: State v. Perdomo is the controlling authority. You must treat its two-pronged test (Characteristics of the Accused / Details of the Interrogation) as the mandatory framework for your discussion.

Precise Issue Spotting

Solid strategy requires a comparison of the new facts (e.g., State v. Hughes) against the precedents established in Perdomo and Mincey.

The Crucial Distinction: The core principle is that a confession cannot be deemed involuntary "Absent some indication of coercive police activity." This means you must separate the defendant's physical weakness (which is not coercive police conduct) from the police methods used.

The Two Prongs: Every relevant fact from the new case must be sorted into either:

Prong 1 (Characteristics): How severely injured, how heavily medicated, the time elapsed since the trauma, and the coherence of their answers.

Prong 2 (Coercion): The officer's tone, the duration of the interview, whether the defendant asked to stop, and if the officers followed hospital instructions.

Key Facts

When reading the File (the new case facts), prioritize collecting details that fall under the Perdomo checklist:

Timing: How long after the injury/surgery was the interview? (Perdomo was 4 days; Mincey was hours).

Medical Status: Was the defendant alert? On a ventilator? What medication had they received, and how long prior?

Defendant's Responses: Was the speech slurred or incoherent? Were the answers detailed and responsive? Did the defendant attempt to deceive the officers? (These facts suggest a "rational intellect.")

Interrogation Details: Exact length of the interview (e.g., 15 minutes, 20 minutes, 3 hours). What was the officers' tone? (e.g., subdued, conversational, threatening). Did the defendant ask to stop?

Structuring the Answer

The Objective Memorandum structure must be rigid and follow this format:

Header: TO, FROM, RE, DATE.

Question Presented: A concise, single-sentence question covering the issue.

Brief Answer: A direct "Yes/No" followed by the core legal rationale (Perdomo's two prongs).

Discussion:

Heading 1: State the governing rule (Totality of Circumstances / Overborne Will).

Sub-Heading 1: Application of Characteristics of the Accused (Prong 1). Contrast the defendant's physical pain with the evidence of their mental acuity (e.g., responsiveness, detailed answers).

Sub-Heading 2: Application of Details of the Interrogation (Coercion) (Prong 2). Focus heavily on the absence of police coercion, comparing the new facts to the non-coercive environment of Perdomo versus the relentless questioning of Mincey.

Step by Step Process

Draft the Header and Preliminary Sections (Q/BA): Dedicate five minutes to setting up the structure perfectly.

Establish the Rule: Write out the Perdomo rule: "rational intellect and free will" and the two-pronged "surrounding circumstances" test.

Analyze Prong 1 (Characteristics): Write a paragraph acknowledging the seriousness of the defendant's injuries and medication (the Mincey similarity). Immediately pivot to the facts proving their mental acuity and volition (e.g., timing days later, clear speech, responsive answers, ability to recall details).

Analyze Prong 2 (Coercion): Write a stronger paragraph establishing that the police activity was non-coercive. Emphasize the short length (15-20 minutes), the conversational/subdued tone, and the absence of any request by the defendant to terminate the interview. Conclude that the confession is voluntary because the police did not overbear the defendant's will.

Final Review: Check the analysis against the two-pronged test. Ensure the conclusion hinges on the lack of police coercion, as Perdomo mandates.

IV. Ultra Concise Answer, Performance Test, February 2023

MEMORANDUM

TO: Supervising Attorney
FROM: Applicant
RE: Admissibility of Hughes's Hospital Statement (Involuntariness Analysis)
DATE: February 22, 2023

QUESTION PRESENTED

Should Hughes's statement, made to police while intubated and heavily medicated in the ICU 36 hours post-surgery, be deemed inadmissible as an involuntary confession under the Due Process Clause?

BRIEF ANSWER

No. The statement is likely admissible.

Although Hughes was seriously injured, the confession was voluntary because the interview was extremely brief, the officers' conduct was non-coercive, and the record demonstrates Hughes retained a rational intellect, consistent with the findings in State v. Perdomo.

DISCUSSION

A statement is involuntary if the totality of the circumstances shows the accused's will was overborne (Perdomo).

Here, the facts, while showing significant pain (Prong 1), do not demonstrate police coercion (Prong 2). Hughes was interviewed 36 hours after trauma, a substantial recovery period unlike the hours-post-injury in Mincey v. Arizona.

Although in the ICU and having received fentanyl one hour prior, Hughes's brief, direct admission ("I was driving") was fully responsive to the officer's single question.

No evidence suggests slurred or incoherent speech. Crucially, the short, 15-minute interview was not relentless, the officer's tone was calm and conversational, and Hughes never requested the questioning cease or asked for counsel, as required to establish police misconduct.

Absent coercive police activity, the statement is not involuntary.

July 2022

California
Bar
Examination

Performance Test
INSTRUCTIONS AND FILE

NIESI v. GOSLING and HARDY

Instructions 2

FILE

Memorandum to Applicant from Carmen Cardinal 5

Excerpts from www.CravenCableConsumersUnited.com Blog 6

Complaint 9

LAW OFFICES OF CARDINAL AND DEETZ

45 Bennington Circle

Craven, Columbia

TO:	**Applicant**
FROM:	**Carmen Cardinal**
RE:	**Niesi v. Gosling and Hardy**
DATE:	**July 26, 2022**

Grace Gosling is the web host of www.CravenCableConsumersUnited.com, a consumer website that contains a blog established to provide a platform for dissatisfied cable customers in Craven, Columbia. Gosling has retained our firm for advice concerning a complaint for defamation filed against her and Hank Hardy, a subscriber and poster to her blog, by Jack Niesi. Niesi claims that both Gosling and Hardy are liable as a result of statements Hardy posted about him to Gosling's blog.

I am preparing to meet with Gosling about Niesi's complaint. To help me prepare for the meeting, please draft an objective memorandum that discusses:

1. Whether Niesi would prove that Hardy's statements, as quoted in the complaint, were defamatory if he were to prove the facts alleged.

2. Whether Gosling is immune from liability for Hardy's allegedly defamatory statements.

Do not draft a separate statement of facts, but use the facts in your discussion.

EXCERPTS

www.CravenCableConsumersUnited.com Blog

Welcome to the voice of cable ratepayers in the City of Craven! I inaugurated this blog to highlight the incompetent and overpriced cable "disservice" and mistreatment we consumers receive as a result of the mismanagement and greed of the tone-deaf colossus, Columbia Cable Company. Despite some government regulation, the lack of competition has nevertheless resulted in poor and costly cable service. It is time to educate ourselves about cable services, our rights as consumers, and ways to contain the cost of cable service. I will be posting information on these topics and invite you to participate by posting anything you think will contribute to these goals. My hope is that members of the community will subscribe to this blog and participate constructively in ongoing discussion and action.

Note: To comment, you must be a subscriber. To subscribe, simply log on and, using the pre-populated pull-down menu, insert your first and last names, full physical address and email address, gender, age, and whether you are a Columbia Cable Company customer. There is also a blank box at the end where you can provide any additional information or comments. Each subscriber will have a profile containing all of this information that is accessible to other subscribers. The profiles will allow you to choose which other subscribers to communicate with outside this blog, including to develop ideas and actions against Columbia Cable Company, organize carpools to and from events, and the like.

In Solidarity, Grace Gosling

Oppose Rate Increase!

On June 27, 2022 at 6:00 p.m., the Craven City Council will hear a request from Columbia Cable Company for a 10% increase in cable rates to subsidize its planned re-cabling and the construction of a new store at the Stratford mall! This comes at a time when we are experiencing further deterioration in customer service with even longer waits on the phone and at the stores to talk to a customer service representative, and bait and switch sales tactics! Be sure to show up all together at the meeting in the Council chambers at Craven City Hall to express your opposition to the rate increase request and to demand better service and ethical sales practices. And if you have any other ideas about how to keep cable costs down, please post them below.

In Solidarity, Grace Gosling

Comments:

Grace: Thanks for starting this very necessary dialogue. I'll tell you a big way to keep down cable rates – report cable theft! I live in the Green Hills condominium complex at 451 Green Hills Drive in Craven. Like most of us, I pay a lot for full cable service while one of my neighbors, Jack Niesi, is guilty of cable theft: He uses various unauthorized devices to get free phone, television and internet service to his condo. I'll bet he isn't even a cable subscriber. It's crooks like Jack Niesi who cause cable costs to go up for the rest of us!

Hank Hardy (June 11, 2022)

Hank: That sounds awful! Can you tell us more?? Have you considered reporting Niesi's theft to the Columbia Cable Company's cable theft hotline?!

In Solidarity, Grace Gosling (June 16, 2022)

Grace: This is further to my June 11, 2022 post about Jack Niesi. Since then, I've been watching him closely. And – get this – while his wife is at work, an attractive young woman is at their house most of the day. It looks as though they are watching TV on his stolen cable service. He appears to be a cheating spouse! I put a note on his wife's car windshield telling that nice woman about her husband's infidelity while she is hard at work. What a loser and low life he is!

Hank Hardy (July 1, 2022)

SUPERIOR COURT OF THE STATE OF COLUMBIA
COUNTY OF MOREHEAD

JACK NIESI, Plaintiff, v. GRACE GOSLING and HANK HARDY, Defendants.	CASE NO: 2022 – 7459 COMPLAINT

1. Plaintiff Jack Niesi is a private individual who at all times mentioned in this complaint was a resident of Morehead County, Columbia.

2. Niesi has worked as an independent television producer for over 20 years and has resided at 451 Green Hills Drive in Craven, Columbia for about 5 years. Niesi has during all this time been faithfully married to his wife, Jill Niesi, and has enjoyed a good reputation, both generally and in his occupation.

3. Defendant Grace Gosling is an individual and is now, and at all times mentioned in this complaint has been, a resident of Morehead County, Columbia. She is the web host of www.CravenCableConsumersUnited.com (3CU.com), which contains a blog. As such, she has unlawfully caused, and is legally responsible for, the injury to Niesi as alleged in this complaint.

4. Defendant Hank Hardy is an individual and is now, and at all times mentioned in this complaint has been, a resident of Morehead County, Columbia. Hardy unlawfully caused, and is legally responsible for, the injury to Niesi as alleged in this complaint.

5. On or about June 11, 2022 and on or about July 1, 2022, Gosling published statements by Hardy on the 3CU.com blog in which Hardy stated:

   a. "I'll tell you a big way to keep down cable rates – report cable theft! I live in the Green Hills condominium complex at 451 Green Hills Drive in Craven. Like most of us, I pay a lot for full cable service while one of my neighbors, Jack Niesi, is guilty of cable theft: He uses various unauthorized devices to get free phone, television and internet service to his condo. I'll bet he isn't even a cable subscriber. It's crooks like Jack Niesi who cause cable costs to go up for the rest of us!"

   b. "Since then [i.e., the date of the statement quoted in Paragraph 5.a.], I've been watching him [i.e., Niesi] closely. And – get this – while his wife is at work, an attractive young woman is at their house most of the day. It looks as though they are watching TV on his stolen cable service. He appears to be a cheating spouse! I put a note on his wife's car windshield telling that nice woman about her husband's infidelity while she is hard at work. What a loser and low life he is!"

6. The statements quoted in Paragraph 5 referred to Niesi by name and address and were so understood by those who read them.

7. The statements quoted in Paragraph 5 are false as they pertain to Niesi. Among other things, Niesi has been a Columbia Cable Company customer for over 20 years. In that entire time, he has paid for every type of cable service he has ever received. He works with his technical assistant, Liana Mabry, from his home office. His relationship with Mabry is, and always has been, purely professional.

8. The statements quoted in Paragraph 5 were seen and read by Niesi's neighbors, business associates, and family, including his wife.

9. As a proximate result of the publication of the statements quoted in Paragraph 5, Niesi has suffered injury in the form of loss of his personal and professional reputation and business, shame, and mortification, all to his damage in a total amount to be established by proof at trial.

WHEREFORE, Niesi demands judgment against Gosling and Hardy, and each of them, as follows:

1. For compensatory damages according to proof;
2. For punitive damages;
3. For interest as allowed by law;
4. For costs of suit; and
5. For such other and further relief as this court may deem just and proper.

DATED: July 22, 2022 ____________*Ella Wang*______________

Ella Wang
Attorney for Jack Niesi

July 2022

California Bar Examination

Performance Test

LIBRARY

NIESI v. GOSLING and HARDY

LIBRARY

Anderson v. Walsh
Columbia Court of Appeal (2013)....................3

Columbia Valley Fair Housing Council v. Roommate.com, LLC
Columbia Court of Appeal (2008)....................7

Anderson v. Walsh

Columbia Court of Appeal (2013)

This case arises from an aborted sale of a wig by Wilma Walsh to Ann Anderson. According to Anderson, Walsh represented that the wig was custom made. Anderson, who works for the City of Astoria Building Department, tendered a check from All Coast Building Contractors, a corporation she and her husband own. After realizing the wig was not custom made, Anderson tried to return the wig via FedEx, but Walsh refused the delivery. Anderson stopped payment on the check. Walsh sued Anderson for breach of contract in small claims court. At trial, Anderson introduced a FedEx document confirming that the package containing the wig had been refused by Walsh. Anderson prevailed in the small claims action.

Thereafter, Walsh authored a lengthy statement about the sale on an online consumer blog on RipOffReport.com. Prefaced by the word "Facts" were two allegedly defamatory statements: (1) "Ann Anderson, who works for the Astoria Building Department, wrote an unauthorized check for a wig from her boyfriend's account and at the bottom wrote that it was for a 'prosthetic donation.'" (2) "Ann Anderson brought to court a made-up document from FedEx stating that Walsh had opened the package, saw what was in it, and gave it back to FedEx." Thereafter, an anonymous author posted the following to the consumer website Yelp.com: "Thank you Ann Anderson of the Astoria Building Department for hurting the community by giving all the construction business in Astoria to family and friends in exchange for bribes. I hope that an investigation takes place soon and that you end up in prison." Though Walsh denied responsibility for the Yelp.com posting, expert testimony tied the email address used in that posting to her.

Upon reading these statements, Anderson was devastated. She felt compelled to report them to her employer and was thereby humiliated and concerned about losing her job. Shortly thereafter, she sued Walsh for defamation based on false statements imputing dishonesty, fraud, and criminal activity. Walsh asserted the affirmative defense of truth. At trial, Anderson proved that the statements were false and the court entered judgment in her favor. On appeal, Walsh asserts that the statements were opinion rather than fact.

In Columbia, defamation consists of the publication of a false statement to a third party, which proximately results in injury to another. To be false, a statement must be one of fact, and cannot be one solely of opinion. If a statement is reasonably susceptible to an interpretation as either fact or opinion, its proper characterization is determined by asking whether, under the totality of the circumstances, a reasonable trier of fact would conclude that the statement communicates actual fact rather than expresses mere opinion.

Walsh claims that her statements concerning Anderson were not defamatory because they were not factual. Relying on our recent decision in *Insky v. Ilston* (Columbia Court of Appeal, 2011), she argues that, even if they were reasonably susceptible to an interpretation as either fact or opinion, a reasonable trier of fact would conclude that they expressed a mere opinion rather than communicated an actual fact under the totality of the circumstances, including that they appeared on consumer websites, where most readers expect to see opinions rather than facts.

In *Insky*, we stated: "Internet forums promote a looser communication style and an outlet for the user to criticize others. Users are able to engage freely in informal debate and criticism, leading many to substitute gossip for accurate reporting and adopt a provocative tone." There, we held that, under the totality of the circumstances, a reasonable trier of fact would conclude that a statement posted online calling company executives "liars, losers, and crooks" expressed mere opinion rather than communicated actual fact. We explained that, "while unquestionably offensive and demeaning" to the executives, the statement was more emotional catharsis than information.

Here, however, things are different. Walsh's statements on RipOffReport.com, which were labeled "facts," recited alleged facts detailing perjury and fraud by Anderson. Walsh's statement on Yelp.com similarly recited alleged facts detailing Anderson's awarding of city contracts to friends and family in exchange for bribes. We do not believe that these statements were reasonably susceptible to an interpretation as mere opinion. But even if they were, we conclude that, under the totality of the circumstances, a reasonable trier of fact would conclude that they communicated actual fact.

AFFIRMED.

Columbia Valley Fair Housing Council v. Roommate.com, LLC

Columbia Court of Appeal (2008)

Defendant Roommate.com, LLC (Roommate) operates a website designed to match people renting spare rooms with people looking for a place to live. It features approximately 150,000 active listings and receives a million page views a day. To post or search listings on Roommate's website, Roommate requires subscribers to create profiles. Roommate also requires subscribers to disclose their gender, sexual orientation, presence of children, and to state their roommate preferences under the same three criteria. Lastly, Roommate encourages subscribers to provide "Additional Comments" about themselves and their desired roommate.

The Columbia Valley Fair Housing Council (Council) sued Roommate for violating housing discrimination laws. The trial court held that Roommate is immune from liability under Section 230 of the General Statutes of Columbia and dismissed the claim. The Council appeals.

The Legislature enacted Section 230 to protect websites from liability for including or failing to remove actionable content in order to preserve the free-flowing nature of internet speech and commerce without unduly prejudicing the enforcement of other important laws. To that end, Section 230 immunizes "interactive computer service providers" from liability arising from content created by third parties. But it does not immunize "information content providers" from liability. Nor does it immunize "interactive computer services providers" from liability to the extent that they act as "information content providers." An "interactive computer service provider" is a person or entity that "enables computer access by multiple users to a computer server." An "information content provider" is a person or entity that "is responsible, in whole or in part, for the creation or development of content." Thus, an "interactive computer service provider" *passively* displays content that may be *actively* created or developed by an "information content provider," whereas an "information content provider" *actively* creates or develops content that may be *passively* displayed by an "interactive computer service provider."

Against this background, we examine whether Roommate is entitled to immunity under Section 230 for the three specific functions the Council alleges violate housing discrimination law.

1. **Roommate's questions to prospective subscribers during the registration process, requiring them to disclose and therefore be subject to discrimination for their gender, family status and sexual orientation**

Because Roommate designed its website registration process around the questionnaire and choice of answers containing discriminatory categories, Roommate is undoubtedly the "information content provider" of the questions and can claim no immunity. Section 230 does not grant immunity for inducing third parties to express illegal preferences.

2. **Roommate's development and display of subscribers' discriminatory preferences**

If an individual queries for a roommate of a particular gender using a search engine that does not contribute to, but provides only neutral tools to carry out, what may be unlawful searches, the search engine has not engaged in "development" for purposes of Section 230. But by requiring subscribers to provide their preferences using a limited set of pre-populated answers *as a condition of accessing its service*, Roommate is more than a passive displayer of information created by others; it becomes, at least in part, a developer of that information. "Discriminatory" questions solicit, and thereby develop, "discriminatory" answers. Here, Roommate designed its search to limit the listing available to subscribers based on gender, sexual orientation, and presence of children. Roommate both elicits the allegedly illegal content and makes use of it in conducting its business. Roommate's work in developing the discriminatory questions, answers, and search mechanism, and in enforcing a system that subjects subscribers to allegedly discriminatory housing practices, renders it an information content provider and, as such, not eligible for immunity under Section 230.

3. Roommate's display of discriminatory statements in the "Additional Comments" section of subscriber profile pages

Roommate encourages subscribers to personalize their profiles by writing additional comments about themselves and their desired roommate in a blank text box at the end of the registration process, and publishes these comments without revision. It is not responsible, in whole or in part, for the development of this content. This is precisely the kind of situation for which Section 230 was designed to provide immunity.

One final note: We must keep in mind that the Legislature enacted Section 230 to protect websites from liability for including or failing to remove actionable content. Close cases must be resolved in favor of immunity lest websites be forced to face death by ten thousand cuts, fighting off a barrage of claims that they created or developed actionable content. Such an interpretation is consistent with the intent of the Legislature to preserve the free-flowing nature of internet speech and commerce without unduly prejudicing the enforcement of other important laws.

REVERSED in part, AFFIRMED in part, and REMANDED.

July 2022 California General Bar Examination Performance Test

PERFORMANCE TEST

II. Concise Outline for the Performance Test, July 2022

The required task is to draft an Objective Memorandum analyzing whether Plaintiff Niesi will prove defamation by Hardy and whether Defendant Gosling is immune from liability under the CDA.

Defamation (Hardy's Liability)

Rule: Defamation requires a false statement of fact. A statement is one of fact, even if susceptible to opinion, if a reasonable trier of fact, considering the totality of the circumstances, would conclude the statement communicates actual fact (Anderson v. Walsh).

Context (Counter-Argument): Online forums promote a "looser communication style" and may lead to statements being classified as non-actionable "emotional catharsis" (Anderson citing Insky).

Statement 1 (Cable Theft):

> **Argument (Fact)**: The statement alleges specific, verifiable criminal misconduct ("guilty of cable theft," "uses various unauthorized devices"). This is akin to the specific fraud/bribery allegations found to be fact in Anderson.
>
> **Conclusion**: Likely a statement of fact, as it is detailed and specific, overcoming the "looser communication" presumption.

Statement 2 (Infidelity/Cheating):

> **Argument (Fact)**: The statement is prefaced with an alleged factual investigation ("I've been watching him closely") and asserts verifiable conduct ("attractive young woman at their house"). The conclusion that he "appears to be a cheating spouse" is based on these specific alleged facts.
>
> **Conclusion**: Likely a statement of fact, as it conveys a factual basis for the assertion of misconduct.
>
> **Overall Prediction**: Niesi is likely to prove the statements were defamatory statements of fact.

CDA § 230 Immunity (Gosling's Liability)

Rule: The Communications Decency Act (§ 230) provides broad immunity to an Interactive Computer Service Provider (ICS) from liability arising from content supplied by a third-party Information Content Provider (ICP).

Exception (Loss of Immunity): Immunity is lost if the ICS provider acts as an ICP by being responsible, in whole or in part, for the creation or development of content (Columbia Valley Fair Housing Council v. Roommate.com, LLC).

Gosling's Role:

Gosling is an ICS Provider (runs the blog platform).

Hardy is the ICP (created the content).

Gosling did not "create or develop" Hardy's specific posts. The blog provides a "blank text box" for subscribers to write "additional comments... without revision."

Distinction from Roommate.com: Loss of immunity in Roommate.com occurred when the platform designed a mandatory system (e.g., pre-populated fields) that induced the specific illegal content (discriminatory preferences). Gosling's general comment box did not induce the specific defamatory remarks.

Close Case Rule: "Close cases must be resolved in favor of immunity" to protect internet commerce.

Overall Prediction: Gosling is likely immune from liability.

III. Comprehensive Guide for the Performance Test, July 2022

Initial Read Through

Task Memo: Immediately identify the document type (Objective Memorandum) and the two issues: (1) Defamation (Fact vs. Opinion) and (2) CDA § 230 Immunity. Note the instruction: "Do not draft a separate statement of facts, but use the facts in your discussion."

File: Quickly skim the blog excerpts and Complaint. Focus on the exact language of the allegedly defamatory statements and the nature of the platform (https://www.google.com/search?q=CravenCableConsumersUnited.com blog, which is a consumer forum).

Library: Quickly identify the legal issues corresponding to the cases: Anderson v. Walsh (Defamation) and Columbia Valley Fair Housing Council (CDA § 230).

Precise Issue Spotting

Issue 1: Defamation (Fact vs. Opinion): This is the core issue. The key is applying the totality of the circumstances test from Anderson to the online statements, balancing the "looser communication style" (from Insky) against the specificity of the factual allegations.

Issue 2: Immunity (ICS vs. ICP): The central question is whether Gosling's passive hosting role crossed the line into being a "developer of content." The answer relies entirely on distinguishing the facts from the mandatory content development system rejected in Roommate.com.

Key Facts

Hardy's Statements: Allege specific, verifiable conduct: (1) "guilty of cable theft" using "unauthorized devices," and (2) "cheating spouse" based on specific observation ("watching him closely," seeing a woman at the condo).

Gosling's Platform: A consumer blog that requires registration but allows subscribers to post "additional comments" in a blank text box without revision.

Parties: Niesi is the Plaintiff (private individual); Hardy is the poster (ICP); Gosling is the web host (ICS Provider).

Structuring the Answer

The Objective Memorandum requires a formal structure:

Header: TO, FROM, RE, DATE.

Question Presented: State the two issues neutrally.

Brief Answer: Provide a concise, one-sentence prediction for each issue (Yes/No answer).

Discussion: Separate discussions for Issue 1 (Defamation) and Issue 2 (Immunity), using clear, rule-based headings.

Step by Step Process

Draft Header, Questions, and Brief Answers: This solidifies the structure.

Draft Discussion I (Defamation):

State the general rule from Anderson (totality of the circumstances/actual fact vs. mere opinion).

Acknowledge the Insky factor (looser online style) but immediately distinguish it.

Apply the rule to both of Hardy's statements. Emphasize the specificity ("unauthorized devices," "watching him closely") to conclude they are statements of fact.

Draft Discussion II (Immunity):

State the § 230 rule: ICS providers are immune for third-party ICP content, unless they develop the content (Roommate.com).

Apply the rule: Gosling is an ICS Provider; Hardy is the ICP.

Distinguish Gosling's passive comment box (protected) from the mandatory, content-inducing system of Roommate.com (not protected).

Conclude with the prediction, noting that close cases favor immunity.

IV. Ultra Concise Answer, Performance Test, July 2022

MEMORANDUM

TO: Carmen Cardinal
FROM: Applicant
RE: Niesi v. Gosling and Hardy
DATE: July 26, 2022

QUESTION PRESENTED

Whether Niesi would prove that Hardy's online statements were defamatory if the facts alleged in the Complaint are proven.

Whether Gosling is immune from liability under the Communications Decency Act (§ 230) for Hardy's allegedly defamatory statements.

BRIEF ANSWER

Yes. Hardy's statements are likely to be deemed specific statements of fact, overcoming the presumption of non-actionable opinion, as they allege verifiable misconduct (Anderson v. Walsh).

Yes. Gosling is likely immune from liability because her role was that of a passive Interactive Computer Service Provider, not a developer of content (Columbia Valley Fair Housing Council v. Roommate.com, LLC).

DISCUSSION

1. Hardy's Statements Constitute Defamatory Facts.

Defamation requires a statement of actual fact, as determined under the totality of the circumstances (Anderson). While the blog context suggests a "looser communication style," Hardy's posts communicate specific, verifiable facts.

The June 11 statement alleging Niesi is "guilty of cable theft" and "uses various unauthorized devices" is specific misconduct, similar to the fraud allegations found to be fact in Anderson.

The July 1 statement, prefaced by the claim of having been "watching him closely" and asserting observations of an attractive woman at his house, gives the impression of a factual investigation, making the "cheating spouse" conclusion a statement of fact based on specific, verifiable conduct.

Niesi will likely prove the statements were defamatory facts.

2. Gosling is Immune from Liability Under CDA § 230.

§ 230 immunizes Interactive Computer Service Providers (ICS) from liability for content provided by third-party Information Content Providers (ICP), unless the ICS is responsible for the "creation or development" of the content (Roommate.com).

Gosling is the ICS, and Hardy is the ICP. Gosling provided a registration system and a "blank text box" for unrevised "additional comments," which Roommate.com found to be protected, passive display.

Gosling did not lose immunity because she did not design a mandatory system that induced the specific defamatory remarks, unlike the discriminatory pre-populated fields in Roommate.com.

Given the statutory directive that close cases be resolved in favor of immunity, Gosling is immune.

February 2022

California
Bar
Examination

Performance Test
INSTRUCTIONS AND FILE

IN RE PRICE

Instructions..

FILE

Memorandum from Debra Uliana to Applicant ....

Transcript of Interview of Mark Price ....

Transcript of Interview of Laila Sayed ....

Office of the District Attorney

County of Dixon

600 Gordon Avenue

Mill Brook, Columbia

MEMORANDUM

TO: Applicant
FROM: Debra Uliana, Chief Deputy District Attorney
DATE: February 22, 2022
RE: In re Price

Last December, the Superior Court dismissed an indictment charging Darryl Howe with murder. It concluded that Deputy District Attorney Mark Price committed prosecutorial misconduct. It found that Price's dealings with Howe on October 3 and November 18, 2021, without the consent of Howe's counsel, violated Howe's privilege against compelled self-incrimination and his right to the assistance of counsel under the Fifth and Sixth Amendments. In dismissing the indictment, the court stated that it had initially considered, but ultimately decided against, referring the matter to the State Bar to investigate whether, in his dealings with Howe on those dates, Price violated Columbia Rule of Professional Conduct 4.2. Rule 4.2, which is commonly referred to as the "no-contact rule," prohibits a lawyer from communicating with a person known to be represented by another lawyer without the other lawyer's consent.

District Attorney Hector Santiago has asked me to draft a proposed policy to assist deputy district attorneys in avoiding violation of Rule 4.2. As a first step, I have interviewed Price and have also interviewed Price's supervisor, Senior Deputy District Attorney Laila Sayed.

Before I begin drafting a proposed policy, I want to know whether, in fact, Price violated Rule 4.2 in his dealings with Howe on October 3 and November 18. To that end, please prepare a memorandum addressing whether Price violated Rule 4.2 in his dealings with Howe on each date, including whether he could rely on Columbia Rule of Professional Conduct 5.2. Rule 5.2 provides that a lawyer does not violate any rule of professional conduct if the lawyer acts in accordance with a supervisor's reasonable resolution of an arguable question of professional duty. Do not include a separate statement of facts in your memorandum, but be sure to use the facts in your analysis.

TRANSCRIPT OF INTERVIEW OF MARK PRICE

February 15, 2022

DEBRA ULIANA: Mark, thanks for sitting for an interview about the *Howe* case.

MARK PRICE: Of course, Debra. We wouldn't have to be going through this exercise if I hadn't botched the case.

ULIANA: Unfortunately, you're not the first deputy to get an indictment dismissed. I'm meeting with you because, in dismissing the indictment, Judge Gorence said she had initially considered referring the matter to the State Bar to investigate whether you violated Rule 4.2, but ultimately decided not to because this was your "first offense" in a long career. I'm meeting with you as a first step in drafting a proposed policy to assist deputy district attorneys in avoiding violation of Rule 4.2.

PRICE: I understand. I'm sorry I've put you and the office in this position.

ULIANA: That's okay. Let's get on with it. I see you've brought the chronology of events I asked you to prepare. Why don't you summarize what happened? I'll ask questions as I need to.

PRICE: Fine. Here we go.

As you know, on August 22, 2021, Billy Wilson was shot and killed in an apartment house here in Mill Brook. Within hours, Darryl Howe was arrested for Wilson's murder. Howe admitted being at the scene of the murder, but claimed he didn't do it.

On August 24, Howe was arraigned in the Superior Court before Judge Gorence. I appeared for the State; Deputy Public Defender James Gardner was appointed to represent Howe; and Howe was ordered held without bond until a preliminary hearing could be held.

On September 6, I moved Judge Gorence to release Howe on his own recognizance pending further investigation of the case. Prior to Howe's release, I told Deputy Public Defender Gardner that I would like to speak with Howe about the case. He said he would consent only if I was willing to offer Howe complete immunity, which of course I was not.

On September 26, Howe called the office of Mill Brook Police Detective Donna Daichi from his home and left a voicemail message saying he wanted to talk to her about the Wilson murder. Detective Daichi immediately told me about the message. I had had no personal experience with a defendant who contacted the police to talk about his own case. I consulted with Senior Deputy District Attorney Laila Sayed, who as you know is my supervisor as the Chief of the Felony Section. She advised me that any statements Howe might volunteer would likely be admissible. She also advised me to instruct Detective Daichi that, if Howe were to call her, she should listen but not ask any questions, and then report what he said to me. I gave those instructions to Detective Daichi.

ULIANA: Mark, did you have any discussion with Laila about Rule 4.2?

PRICE: Yes. I don't remember whether I raised the issue or whether Laila did. But I'm sure she told me Rule 4.2 permitted prosecutors to communicate with defendants known to be represented by counsel without counsel's consent, so long as they are conducting an investigation.

ULIANA: Okay. Did Howe call Detective Daichi after September 26?

PRICE: Yes, he called her from his home on October 3. He made several statements to her about the Wilson murder. As I had instructed her, she listened but did not ask any questions, and reported to me what he said.

ULIANA: And then?

PRICE: And then, on October 5, Judge Gorence conducted a preliminary hearing, found probable cause to charge Howe with the Wilson murder, and remanded him to custody and ordered him held without bond. At the preliminary hearing, Deputy Public Defender Gardner learned of the events of October 3 and asked Judge Gorence to order Detective Daichi not to speak with Howe. Judge Gorence declined to do so, but observed that Gardner would undoubtedly instruct Howe that such dealings were not in his best interest.

On October 19, the grand jury handed up the indictment charging Howe with the Wilson murder.

Then, about a month later, on November 18, while Detective Daichi was in my office working with me on the Wilson murder case, I received a collect call from Howe from the jail on my private line. I accepted the call. I hadn't given Howe my number; he must have gotten it from Daichi. At my request, Daichi listened in on an extension. Although I advised Howe that he did not have to speak with me and that Deputy Public Defender Gardner would not be happy if he did, he nevertheless proceeded to talk about the Wilson murder for about 20 minutes while Daichi and I listened and took notes.

ULIANA: Any further discussion with Laila about Rule 4.2 around November 18?

PRICE: Probably the same as before, that Rule 4.2 permitted prosecutors conducting an investigation to communicate with defendants known to be represented by counsel without counsel's consent.

ULIANA: And then?

PRICE: Finally, as you know, on December 8, Judge Gorence held a hearing at the request of Deputy Public Defender Gardner. By this time, Gardner had learned of the events of November 18. Gardner moved to dismiss the indictment for what he claimed was prosecutorial misconduct. Unfortunately, Judge Gorence granted the motion. And the rest is history.

ULIANA: Yes, Mark. Sad to say, it is. You've given me a good introduction. If I need to follow up, I'll let you know.

PRICE: Fine. Again, I'm sorry about all of this.

ULIANA: I understand. We've all got to be more careful in the future.

TRANSCRIPT OF INTERVIEW OF LAILA SAYED

February 18, 2022

DEBRA ULIANA: Laila, thanks for coming for an interview about the *Howe* case.

LAILA SAYED: No problem.

ULIANA: You've had a chance to review any materials you might believe are relevant?

SAYED: Yes, but I must add that there were few such materials. In the Felony Section, we don't have much time to commit anything to paper.

ULIANA: I understand. Let me cut to the chase and ask about your discussions with Mark Price about the *Howe* case.

SAYED: Ready when you are.

ULIANA: Do you recall Mark consulting you, on September 26 of last year, after Howe had contacted Mill Brook Police Detective Donna Daichi and had made statements to her about the Wilson murder?

SAYED: Yes. Although I can't swear that we spoke on September 26, I remember we spoke about Howe's statements to Detective Daichi.

ULIANA: Do you recall Mark telling you something to the effect that he had had no personal experience with a defendant who contacted the police to discuss his own case?

SAYED: Yes.

ULIANA: Do you recall speaking with Mark about the admissibility of any statements Howe might make to Detective Daichi?

SAYED: Yes. I probably told him that any statements Howe might volunteer would likely be admissible.

ULIANA: Do you recall speaking with Mark about Detective Daichi's interactions with Howe?

SAYED: Yes. I probably told Mark to tell Detective Daichi to listen to Howe if he contacted her again, but not to ask him any questions, and to report to Mark what Howe said.

ULIANA: Why?

SAYED: To make sure any statements would be admissible.

ULIANA: Do you recall speaking with Mark about Rule 4.2, the no-contact rule?

SAYED: No.

ULIANA: You don't recall telling him that the no-contact rule or Rule 4.2 permitted prosecutors to communicate with defendants known to be represented by counsel without counsel's consent, so long as they are conducting an investigation?

SAYED: No.

ULIANA: Are you sure?

SAYED: Yes, I'm sure.

ULIANA: Why?

SAYED: Debra, you know that we have to refer any non-trivial question about professional conduct to Senior Deputy District Attorney Lamar Lewis, the Compliance Officer. And dealing with a defendant who is known to be represented by counsel without counsel's consent is certainly a non-trivial question. Had Mark raised any question about the no-contact rule with me, I would have referred it to Lamar. I didn't refer it to Lamar. That means that Mark didn't raise it with me.

ULIANA: Let's proceed to November 18. Do you recall Mark consulting you around that date, for a second time, about Howe and his statements to Mark as well as Detective Daichi?

SAYED: No. After speaking with Mark in September about Howe and his statements to Detective Daichi, I did not speak with him about the matter again, at least not before Judge Gorence dismissed the indictment. After Judge Gorence dismissed the indictment, as I believe you know, I had a long and unpleasant "discussion" with Mark about the matter.

ULIANA: Yes, I know about the "discussion." But you're sure you don't recall a second consultation on or around November 18?

SAYED: I'm sure. In my 20 years in the office, I've never heard of a defendant contacting a deputy district attorney. Had Mark told me that Howe had contacted him, I would have immediately referred the matter to Lamar Lewis. And I would certainly have remembered it.

ULIANA: Well, Laila, you've answered the questions I have now. If more occur to me, I'll let you know. Thanks.

SAYED: You're welcome.

February 2022

California
Bar
Examination

Performance Test
LIBRARY

IN RE PRICE

LIBRARY

Selected Columbia Rules of Professional Conduct..

State v. Nelson
Columbia Supreme Court (2015)...

SELECTED COLUMBIA RULES OF PROFESSIONAL CONDUCT

Rule 4.2. Communication with a Represented Person

(a) In representing a client, a lawyer shall not communicate directly or indirectly about the subject of the representation with a person the lawyer knows to be represented by another lawyer in the matter, unless the lawyer has the consent of the other lawyer.

. . . . .

(c) This rule shall not prohibit: (1) communications with a public official, board, committee, or body; or (2) communications otherwise authorized by law or a court order.

. . . . .

Comment

[1] This rule applies even though the represented person initiates or consents to the communication. . . .

. . . . .

[2] The prohibition against communicating "indirectly" with a person represented by counsel in paragraph (a) is intended to address situations where a lawyer seeks to communicate with a represented person through an intermediary such as an agent, investigator or the lawyer's client.

. . . . .

[3] Paragraph (c)(2) recognizes that statutory schemes, case law, and court orders may authorize communications between a lawyer and a person that would otherwise be subject to this rule. The law recognizes that

> prosecutors and other government lawyers are authorized to contact represented persons, either directly or through investigative agents and informants, in the context of investigative activities, as limited by relevant federal and state constitutions, statutes, rules, and case law. The rule is not intended to preclude communications with represented persons in the course of such legitimate investigative activities as authorized by law.

. . . . .

* * * * *

Rule 5.2. Responsibilities of a Subordinate Lawyer

(a) A lawyer shall comply with these rules notwithstanding that the lawyer acts at the direction of another lawyer or other person.

(b) A subordinate lawyer does not violate these rules if that lawyer acts in accordance with a supervisory lawyer's reasonable resolution of an arguable question of professional duty.

Comment

When lawyers in a supervisor-subordinate relationship encounter a matter involving professional judgment as to the lawyers' responsibilities under these rules and the question can reasonably be answered only one way, the duty of both lawyers is clear and they are equally responsible for fulfilling it. Accordingly, the subordinate lawyer must comply with his or her obligations under paragraph (a). If the question reasonably can be answered more than one way, the supervisory lawyer may assume responsibility for determining which of the reasonable alternatives to select, and the subordinate may be guided accordingly. . . .

State v. Nelson

Columbia Supreme Court (2015)

We granted review in this case to address the question whether a prosecutor violates Rule 4.2 of the Columbia Rules of Professional Conduct, which is commonly referred to as the no-contact rule, by communicating, post-indictment, with a defendant known to be represented by counsel, without counsel's consent. The answer, as will appear, is yes.

FACTUAL BACKGROUND AND PROCEDURAL HISTORY

James Nelson and Philip Brooks were indicted for conspiracy to distribute cocaine in the Superior Court of the County of Pleasanton. Nelson retained attorney Barry Tarlow to represent him, and Brooks retained attorney James Young.

While awaiting trial, Nelson was detained with Brooks at the Pleasanton County Jail. Tarlow informed Nelson that he believed that he and Brooks had a viable entrapment defense and that, in any case, it was his general policy not to negotiate a plea agreement with the State at this stage in the proceedings.

Young had agreed with Tarlow to coordinate a joint investigation. In so doing, Young often spoke to both Nelson and Brooks by telephone and in person during visits to Pleasanton.

One day, Nelson and Brooks telephoned Young and expressed an interest in negotiating a plea agreement. Without informing Tarlow, Young twice traveled to Pleasanton in order to discuss negotiating a plea agreement with Nelson and Brooks. Nelson asked Brooks and Young not to reveal their discussions to Tarlow because he feared that, if Tarlow learned that he was involved in negotiating a plea agreement, Tarlow would withdraw as his counsel and thereby deprive him of his services in the event the case were to go to trial.

Young contacted Deputy District Attorney Joan Lyons, who was prosecuting the case against Nelson and Brooks, on behalf of both men. Subsequently, along with Brooks and Young, Nelson met with Lyons twice in her office. Following the second meeting, Lyons sent Young a proposed plea agreement for Nelson and Brooks. After talking with Young, Nelson and Brooks rejected the proposal.

Not long thereafter, Tarlow discovered what had transpired and filed a motion to dismiss the indictment. Tarlow alleged that Lyons violated the Sixth Amendment, which granted Nelson the right to Tarlow's assistance, and also violated Columbia Rule of Professional Conduct 4.2, which prohibited her from communicating with Nelson without Tarlow's consent. After a hearing, the Superior Court concluded that Lyons did not violate the Sixth Amendment, since Nelson was not deprived of Tarlow's assistance. But it also concluded that she did indeed violate Rule 4.2. In the exercise of its supervisory powers, it dismissed the indictment against Nelson.

The State appealed from the dismissal. The Court of Appeal, however, affirmed. The State petitioned for review. We granted review, and now affirm the Court of Appeal's affirmance.

DISCUSSION

The State does not dispute that, *if* Lyons violated Rule 4.2, the Superior Court properly dismissed the indictment against Nelson in the exercise of its supervisory power. The State claims only that Lyons did not violate Rule 4.2.

In support, the State argues that Rule 4.2 was not intended to apply to a prosecutor. It is too late in the day to present such an argument. Years ago, we held that a "prosecutor is no less subject to the Columbia Rules of Professional Conduct than any other lawyer." *State v. Mann* (Columbia Supreme Ct., 1976). It is true that, depending on the circumstances, a prosecutor may or may not be prohibited from communicating with a defendant known to be represented by counsel, without counsel's consent, *before the defendant is indicted.* Such circumstances include whether the prosecutor knows that the defendant has expressed a willingness to communicate, a fact that would militate in favor of communication, and whether the prosecutor knows that counsel has expressed an unwillingness to consent, a fact that would militate against communication. But it is also true that, in all circumstances, a prosecutor is prohibited from communicating with a defendant known to be represented by counsel, without counsel's consent, *after the defendant has been indicted*. Indictment gives rise to a defendant's Sixth Amendment right to rely upon counsel as a medium between him and the State. The defendant's Sixth Amendment right would be meaningless if one of its critical components, a lawyer-client relationship characterized by trust and confidence, could be circumvented by a prosecutor under the guise of conducting an investigation.

The State then argues that Rule 4.2 does not prohibit a prosecutor from communicating with a defendant known to be represented by counsel, without counsel's consent, *if the prosecutor is conducting an investigation*. The State relies on Comment [8] to Rule 4.2, which states that "[t]he rule is not intended to preclude communications with represented persons in the course of … legitimate investigative activities as authorized by law." We read Comment [8] to mean that a prosecutor is not prohibited from communicating with a represented defendant *if and to the extent that the prosecutor is authorized by law to do so*. In Columbia, however, a prosecutor is *not* authorized by law to communicate with a represented defendant where, as here, the defendant has been indicted.

Finally, the State next argues that, even if Rule 4.2 prohibits a prosecutor from communicating with a defendant known to be represented by counsel without counsel's consent, it prohibits a prosecutor only from *speaking* and not from *listening*. While certainly one purpose of Rule 4.2 is to prevent attorneys from utilizing their legal skills to gain an advantage over an unsophisticated lay person, an equally important purpose is to protect a person represented by counsel not only from the approaches of his or her adversary's lawyer, but from the folly of his or her own well-meaning initiatives and the generally unfortunate consequences of his or her ignorance.

CONCLUSION

Because Lyons did indeed violate Rule 4.2, the Superior Court properly dismissed the indictment against Nelson in the exercise of its supervisory powers.

And because the Superior Court properly dismissed the indictment against Nelson, the judgment of the Court of Appeal affirming the dismissal must be, and hereby is,

AFFIRMED.

February 2022 California General Bar Examination Performance Test

II. Concise Outline for the Performance Test, February 2022

A. Rule 4.2 Violation: October 3 Communication (Indirect Contact)

Issue: Did Price violate Rule 4.2 by indirectly communicating with Howe, a represented defendant, on October 3?

Rule 4.2(a): Prohibits a lawyer from communicating indirectly with a represented person about the subject of representation without consent.

Indirect Communication: Price used Detective Daichi as an intermediary/agent. Comment [2] explicitly prohibits this.

Exception (Rule 4.2(c)(2) & Comment [3]): Allows communications "authorized by law" for legitimate investigative activities.

State v. Nelson: Establishes that post-indictment, a prosecutor is prohibited from communicating with a represented defendant, even under the guise of an investigation.

Application: Though Howe was not yet indicted (only arrested/arraigned), the facts show Price's involvement was beyond passive listening. Price actively instructed Daichi to act as an agent to collect information. This indirect, active involvement violates the spirit and text of Rule 4.2(a), even pre-indictment, as Price sought to bypass counsel after Gardner explicitly refused consent.

Conclusion: Likely a violation.

B. Rule 4.2 Violation: November 18 Communication (Direct Contact)

Issue: Did Price violate Rule 4.2 by directly communicating with Howe, a represented and indicted defendant, on November 18?

Rule 4.2(a) & Comment [1]: Prohibits direct communication, even though the represented person (Howe) initiates or consents to the call.

Post-Indictment Prohibition: Howe had been indicted (October 19). State v. Nelson is controlling: post-indictment, a prosecutor is prohibited from communicating with the represented defendant in all circumstances, even for investigation. The Sixth Amendment right takes precedence.

Listening vs. Speaking: The State's argument that 4.2 only prohibits speaking is rejected by Nelson, which holds that Rule 4.2 protects the represented person from the "folly of his or her own well-meaning initiatives." Price listened and took notes for 20 minutes; this is prohibited communication.

Conclusion: Clear violation.

C. Rule 5.2 Defense (Subordinate Reliance)

Issue: Can Price rely on Rule 5.2 to shield him from liability for violating Rule 4.2?

Rule 5.2(b): Requires the subordinate lawyer (Price) to act in accordance with a supervisor's (Sayed's) reasonable resolution of an arguable question of professional duty.

Requirement 1 (Supervisor's Resolution): Price claims Sayed advised him that Rule 4.2 permitted contact for investigation. Sayed flatly denies advising him on Rule 4.2 at all, stating she would have referred it to the Compliance Officer. This creates a factual dispute.

Requirement 2 (Arguable Question): The question regarding pre-indictment contact (Oct. 3) was arguable, depending on the facts, per Nelson's discussion of pre-indictment circumstances. However, the question of post-indictment contact (Nov. 18) is not arguable; Nelson states, "in all circumstances, a prosecutor is prohibited" post-indictment.

Requirement 3 (Reasonable Resolution): Sayed's purported advice that the rule always permits contact for investigation is unreasonable, especially post-indictment, as it directly contradicts Nelson.

Conclusion: Price fails the Rule 5.2 defense for the November 18 violation because the question was not "arguable" post-indictment. He likely fails for October 3 as Sayed denies the advice and the advice itself was arguably unreasonable given the duty to consult the compliance officer for non-trivial questions.

III. Comprehensive Guide for the Performance Test, February 2022

Initial Read Through

Task Memo: Immediately identify the CALLS (Violation of Rule 4.2 on Oct. 3? Violation of Rule 4.2 on Nov. 18? Reliance on Rule 5.2?) and the FORMAT (Objective Memorandum, no separate facts section). This sets up the three primary legal sections required in the final answer.

Library (Rules and Case): Start here to establish the legal framework.

Key terms to highlight:

Rule 4.2: "directly or indirectly," "knows to be represented," "unless authorized by law."

Rule 5.2: "subordinate lawyer," "supervisory lawyer's reasonable resolution of an arguable question."

Nelson: The core holding that post-indictment contact is prohibited in all circumstances (this is the key rule for the Nov. 18 issue). Note its discussion of pre-indictment contact for the Oct. 3 issue.

File (Facts): Read the transcripts specifically looking for:

The precise status of Howe on Oct. 3 (pre-indictment) vs. Nov. 18 (post-indictment).

Who initiated the contact on each date (Howe initiated both).

Price's actions (instructed Daichi to listen; accepted collect call and listened for 20 minutes).

The factual dispute between Price (Sayed gave 4.2 advice) and Sayed (denied giving 4.2 advice).

Precise Issue Spotting

Rule 4.2 (October 3): Was Price's indirect communication (using Daichi) permissible pre-indictment, given his active instruction to Daichi to listen?

Rule 4.2 (November 18): Was Price's direct communication (accepting the collect call) permissible post-indictment, given Howe's initiation and the Nelson rule?

Rule 5.2: Did Price receive a reasonable resolution from Sayed on an arguable question? This requires analyzing the factual dispute and the reasonableness of the advice against the Nelson precedent.

Key Facts

October 3: Howe was only arraigned/pre-indictment. Price instructed Daichi to "listen but not ask any questions." Gardner had already denied consent.

November 18: Howe was indicted (Oct. 19) and was in custody/jail. Howe initiated the collect call. Price accepted and listened for 20 minutes while taking notes.

Rule 5.2 Defense: Price claims Sayed gave Rule 4.2 advice; Sayed denies it and states any non-trivial question should be referred to the Compliance Officer (Lamar Lewis), confirming the office protocol suggests the matter was non-trivial.

Structuring the Answer

The answer must be structured as an Objective Memorandum addressing the three issues in the order requested by the Task Memo. Use strong, underlined headings for clear organization.

Format:

TO/FROM/DATE/RE (Formal Memo Header)

Introduction/Conclusion Summary (Briefly state whether Price violated the rules and whether the defense applies).

Heading 1: Analysis of October 3 Violation

Heading 2: Analysis of November 18 Violation

Heading 3: Analysis of Rule 5.2 Defense

Step by Step Process for Answering

Header: Draft the TO/FROM/DATE/RE header immediately.

Issue 1 (October 3):

Rule: State the general rule (4.2(a)) and the "indirect" prohibition (Comment [2]).

Counter-Rule: Introduce the investigative exception (4.2(c)(2) and Comment [3]).

Analysis: Apply the facts (pre-indictment, Daichi as agent, Price's instructions) and distinguish from the Nelson post-indictment rule. Conclude by arguing that Price's proactive instructions likely constitute an indirect violation aimed at circumventing counsel.

Issue 2 (November 18):

Rule: State the Rule 4.2 prohibition, noting that initiation/consent is irrelevant (Comment [1]).

Nelson Rule: State the clear, non-negotiable rule from State v. Nelson: post-indictment, a prosecutor is prohibited from communicating in all circumstances.

Analysis: Apply the facts (post-indictment, accepted collect call, listened for 20 minutes) and use the Nelson reasoning (protection from the folly of own initiatives). Conclude: Clear Violation.

Issue 3 (Rule 5.2 Defense):

Rule: State Rule 5.2(b): subordinate acting on supervisor's reasonable resolution of an arguable question.

Analysis: Break down the analysis:

November 18: Not an arguable question because Nelson is controlling law prohibiting post-indictment contact. Defense Fails.

October 3: The question may have been arguable, but Price fails on the resolution (Sayed denies giving advice) and reasonableness (the advice Price claims contradicts Nelson's principles and Sayed admitted the issue was non-trivial/referrable).

Conclusion: Rule 5.2 cannot shield Price from either violation.

Review: Ensure the answer is an objective memo format, does not have a separate fact section, and is concise (target $250-325$ words) while hitting all legal points.

IV. Ultra Concise Answer, Performance Test, February 2022

TO: Debra Uliana, Chief Deputy District Attorney
FROM: Applicant
DATE: October 18, 2025
RE: Mark Price's Violations of Rule 4.2 and Rule 5.2 Defense

Conclusion

Deputy District Attorney Mark Price violated Columbia Rule of Professional Conduct 4.2 in his dealings with Darryl Howe on both October 3 and November 18, 2021. He cannot rely on Rule 5.2 because the November 18 question was not arguable, and the supervisory advice for the October 3 contact is factually disputed and unreasonable.

October 3 Rule 4.2 Violation (Pre-Indictment Contact)

Rule 4.2(a) prohibits a lawyer from indirectly communicating with a represented person without counsel's consent. Comment [2] states this includes using an agent, such as Detective Daichi, to speak with Howe about the murder. Although Howe initiated the call pre-indictment, Price actively instructed Daichi to "listen but not ask any questions," establishing an agency relationship to circumvent counsel who had already denied consent. While Comment [3] allows investigative activity, Price's orchestrated communication constitutes an indirect violation of 4.2(a).

November 18 Rule 4.2 Violation (Post-Indictment Contact)

Price clearly violated Rule 4.2 on November 18. Rule 4.2 Comment [1] states the prohibition applies even if the represented person initiates or consents, which Howe did by placing the collect call. Crucially, Howe was indicted on October 19. State v. Nelson is controlling, holding that post-indictment, a prosecutor is prohibited from communicating with a represented defendant in all circumstances to protect the defendant's Sixth Amendment right. Price's acceptance and 20 minutes of listening/note-taking constitutes prohibited communication.

Rule 5.2 Defense

Price cannot rely on Rule 5.2(b), which shields a subordinate acting on a supervisor's reasonable resolution of an arguable question of professional duty. The November 18 contact was not an arguable question because Nelson explicitly and absolutely prohibits post-indictment contact. Furthermore, Sayed denies providing any Rule 4.2 advice to Price, stating the issue was non-trivial and would have been referred to the Compliance Officer, undercutting Price's claim that he was relying on a reasonable supervisory resolution.

July 2021

California
Bar
Examination

Performance Test

INSTRUCTIONS AND FILE

INDUSTRIAL SANDBLASTING, INC. v. MORGAN

Instructions ....

FILE

Memorandum from Sylvia Baca to Applicant ....

Excerpt from Transcript of Testimony of Samuel Morgan ....

Excerpt from Transcript of Testimony of Roger Cole ....

Contract between Industrial Sandblasting, Inc.
and Samuel Morgan (Excerpt) ....

Sylvia Baca and Associates, P.C.
2343 Whitetail Road
Columbia City, Columbia

MEMORANDUM

TO: Applicant
FROM: Sylvia Baca
DATE: July 27, 2021
RE: Industrial Sandblasting, Inc. v. Samuel Morgan

The firm represents Samuel Morgan, who works as a sandblaster and bid manager for Columbia Coatings Corporation. Until about three months ago, Morgan worked for a competitor named Industrial Sandblasting, Inc. (Industrial). Morgan had a contract with Industrial that contained a covenant not to compete if Morgan ever left Industrial.

Industrial has sued Morgan for breach of contract. Industrial wants to enjoin him from doing any work at all at Columbia Coatings for one year. We agreed to a bench trial and held a hearing three weeks ago. I attach transcripts of the relevant portions of testimony at that hearing. I also attach the relevant provisions of the contract between Morgan and Industrial, dated February 15, 2016.

The judge has scheduled us for closing argument on whether the covenants are valid. Please prepare a draft of the oral argument that I might present, using the attached cases as authority.

Excerpt of Transcript from Hearing
Industrial Sandblasting, Inc. v. Samuel Morgan

Held on July 6, 2021

Testimony of Samuel Morgan

. . . . .

Att'y Baca: When did you start work at Industrial Sandblasting, Inc.?

Morgan: In February 2013.

Baca: What did you do for Industrial?

Morgan: I specialize in commercial sandblasting. For several years, I operated a crew and did estimates for my old employer, Industrial Sandblasting, Inc.

Baca: Describe what commercial sandblasting means.

Morgan: We take paint and rust off of buildings, industrial equipment, pipelines, that kind of thing. Then we recoat them with a more durable covering.

Baca: How much did Industrial pay you at the start?

Morgan: They offered me $35,000 per year and I was glad to get it.

Baca: Did you have experience?

Morgan: No. It was entry-level, with no contract. They offered on-the-job training.

Baca: What happened after you got hired?

Morgan: They started me off with the simplest equipment. I figured that out pretty quickly and eventually learned how to operate all of the equipment. I got so good that different foremen would ask for me for the harder jobs.

Baca: How did your responsibilities change after those first few years?

Morgan: About five years ago. The company decided that it would help their business if they could advertise that they had people with certain kinds of certifications. So they paid me while I obtained certifications from the Society for Protective Coatings (SPC), starting six years ago. The SPC has different levels of certification, all labelled QP. In the end, I got a QP1 for external structures, a QP2 for removing hazardous coatings, a QP6 for applying metalized coatings, and a QP8 for coating concrete with polymer.

Baca: How long did that take you?

Morgan: A few months for each certification. I would find a course that introduced me to how to handle the particular task, then worked with the company to make sure that it had the equipment and management to meet SPC standards. Then we'd apply. An auditor would come and spend a week or so making sure of our capacity, and then we'd get the certification.

Baca: How did it help Industrial's business?

Morgan: We started to get a lot of different kinds of jobs, and a lot of different regular customers, mostly because we could handle a bigger range of work.

Baca: What other responsibilities did you take on?

Morgan: One year, I took over from the foreman of that crew who got sick and couldn't continue. So the company asked me to take over. I got it done early and under estimate. Both the town and the company were very satisfied. Industrial kept me with that team and promoted me to team manager.

Baca: What happened after that?

Morgan: My work was always on time and on budget and my people were always happy. One day, someone I knew in the home office asked me to help him put together a bid, as well as an estimate. He wanted to figure out how to make lower bids, and he knew that I had figured out how to do it.

Baca: How did that work out?

Morgan: It worked out well. Eventually the boss, Roger Cole, called me in and said that they couldn't promote me to the office, because they needed me in the field. But Cole also said that they wanted to keep me, so he offered me a raise and a contract. I accepted. It was good money.

Baca: Is that the contract they say you've broken?

Morgan: Yes. We signed it around 5 years ago.

Baca: What happened after you signed?

Morgan: Pretty much the same as before, except I was paid more. I kept bouncing between doing jobs and helping with estimates. Eventually, it became a strain.

Baca: Why?

Morgan: After the contract, I never got another raise. And he kept pushing me to take on more jobs. That was fine for my team; they got overtime. But I was on salary, which stopped going up.

Baca: At that point, what did you know about Columbia Coatings?

Morgan: Columbia Coatings started up about three years ago, but they were very aggressive about bidding, and often took jobs away from us – not always, but enough to notice. They never got one of my customers. Eventually, I got a call from them.

Baca: What did they say?

Morgan: They were up front. They said that they wanted to get more business, and they knew that I was valuable to Cole and Industrial. They asked whether I would come to work with them instead. I told them my problem with Cole, and they said no problem. They said that they would pay me $20,000 more, give me an office position, and let me work in the field as much or as little as I wanted.

Baca: When did this conversation occur?

Morgan: About three months ago. I thought it over, then let them know that I would accept. I gave Cole two weeks notice and left.

Baca: How did Cole take it?

Morgan: He was angry. He asked where I was going, and he got angrier. He made all kinds of threats and cursed me out. He said I'd regret making this decision and that I'd never work in the industry again.

Baca: Just a few more questions. When you worked for Industrial, you said you worked only in Columbia City. Is that right?

Morgan: I did one job in Sidalia, in the northeast part of the state. I did one job in Crescent, a suburb about 20 miles from Columbia City. Otherwise, all the work was in Columbia City, in the northwest corner of the state.

Baca: Where does Columbia Coatings want you to work?

Morgan: I have jobs in the south and southeast. And my office work deals with work all over the state.

Baca: How long will it take Industrial to replace you?

Morgan: They hired another foreman the week before I left. They already had someone doing the bidding – the man in the home office who asked me to help with bids and estimates. He knew pretty much what I knew.

Baca: What would happen if the court applies the non-compete clause to you?

Morgan: I won't have any work at all, after years of experience in the field.

Baca: No further questions.

Att'y Rice: Cross-examination, Your Honor?

Judge Yan: Go ahead.

Rice: You learned everything you knew about sandblasting at Industrial. Isn't that right, Mr. Morgan?

Morgan: Yes.

Rice: They invested a lot in getting you trained and qualified, didn't they?

Morgan: No. They didn't.

Rice: They paid you to get trained, didn't they?

Morgan: No. I paid for the QP certifications myself; all they did was let me do some of the coursework during work hours. It didn't cost much, but Cole sure didn't pay out for it.

Rice: Without you, Industrial won't be able to use those certificates, will it?

Morgan: Wrong again. By now, other foremen have gotten certified. Industrial won't miss me.

Rice: Columbia Coatings doesn't have any of these certifications?

Morgan: They do not. But they have foremen who do.

Rice: You learned how to estimate job costs at Industrial, didn't you?

Morgan: Yes, I did.

Rice: And now you want to use that to harm Industrial, isn't that right?

Morgan: I just want a job that pays me what I'm worth.

Rice: No further questions.

Excerpt of Transcript from Hearing
Industrial Sandblasting Inc. v. Samuel Morgan

Held on July 6, 2021

Testimony of Roger Cole

. . . . .

Att'y Rice: What impact will Mr. Morgan's working at Columbia Coatings have on your business?

Cole: A big impact. Morgan was a key employee, especially when it came to pricing out jobs. He's bringing them expertise that we trained him to have. We can already see the effect it's having.

Rice: What do you mean?

Cole: We have lost several bids to Columbia Coatings already – bids we wouldn't have lost if Morgan weren't there.

Rice: You say that you trained him to have his current expertise. What do you mean?

Cole: We paid him for the days that he attended the QP certification courses. We gave him the work that let him figure out how to price jobs. We provided him with the support and equipment to work his projects. He got all of that while working for us.

Rice: What do you want this court to do?

Cole: Enforce the contract, keep him from working in the industry for one year, anywhere in Columbia.

Rice: Is that all?

Cole: At a minimum, the court should keep him out of Columbia City, at least for long enough for us to train someone the way we trained him.

Rice: You would accept that change?

Cole: Yes. He agreed to what's in the contract, so he ought to accept less.

Rice: No further questions.

Baca: No cross-examination, Your Honor.

Employment Contract

The parties to this contract are Industrial Sandblasting, Inc. ("Employer") and Samuel Morgan ("Employee").

. . . . .

11. For a period of one (1) year after the termination of Employee's employment for any reason, Employee will not own, operate, or work at any business in direct competition with Employer by providing sandblasting or similar industrial cleaning services to industries and businesses anywhere in the State of Columbia.

. . . . .

____
Samuel Morgan, Employee

February 15, 2016
Date

____
Michelle Abebe, President
Industrial Sandblasting, Inc.

February 15, 2016
Date

July 2021

California
Bar
Examination

Performance Test
LIBRARY

INDUSTRIAL SANDBLASTING, INC. v. MORGAN

LIBRARY

Strom v. Knox Broadcasting Corporation
Columbia Supreme Court (2014) ....

Fawcett Railway Relief, Inc. v. Columbia Rail Services, Inc.
Columbia Court of Appeal (2015)..

Strom v. Knox Broadcasting Corporation

Columbia Supreme Court (2014)

This appeal arises from a trial court decision upholding the non-compete provisions of an employment contract between George Strom and Knox Broadcasting Corporation. Strom left Knox Broadcasting Corporation to work for a competing broadcaster, WCAP-TV. WCAP-TV brought the action below to invalidate the non-compete provision and permit Strom to appear on air for WCAP-TV.

The trial court findings indicate that, from 2008 until 2013, George Strom was employed by Knox Broadcasting Corporation ("Knox") as a meteorologist and "television personality." That contract ended on September 1, 2013 and included the following contractual provision:

> Employee shall not, for a period of one hundred-eighty (180) days after the end of the Term of Employment, allow his/her voice or image to be broadcast 'on air' by any commercial television station whose broadcast transmission tower is located within a radius of thirty-five (35) miles from Company's offices in Columbia City, Columbia.

During Strom's employment with Knox, Knox spent in excess of a million dollars promoting Strom's name, voice, and image as an individual television personality and as part of Knox's Action News Team. Strom is one of the most recognized television personalities in the Columbia City area. Local television personalities are strongly identified in the minds of television viewers with the stations upon which they appear.

In April 2013, Strom entered into a five-year contractual agreement with WCAP–TV, a competitor of Knox, to work for WCAP as a meteorologist and "television personality" when his contract with Knox expired.

After learning of Strom's prospective departure, Knox instituted a "transition plan" to reduce the impact Strom's departure would have on the station's image. That plan depended on Strom not appearing on air for WCAP-TV for at least six months after leaving Knox. To permit Strom to appear on air for WCAP-TV during those six months would disrupt Knox's plans for a transition to a replacement for Strom.

Strom's contract with WCAP-TV does not require him to appear "on air" during the first six months of his employment. Under this contract, Strom would perform substantial duties and services to WCAP–TV for which he is being compensated. To permit Strom to appear on air, WCAP-TV would take advantage of the substantial investment Knox had put into developing Strom's public persona, in which Knox had a legitimate and protectable interest.

Finally, Strom will suffer no financial harm from staying off the air during the six months following his departure from Knox.

This case requires us to apply Columbia Stat. Ann. § 24-6-53(a), which states in relevant part:

> (a) Enforcement of contracts that restrict competition during the term of a restrictive covenant, so long as such restrictions are reasonable in time, geographic area, and scope of prohibited activities, shall be permitted.

The statute applies to contracts between employers and employees and thus applies to the contract between Strom and Knox.

Under the statute, we should uphold such a covenant only when strictly limited in time, territorial effect, and scope of the prohibited activities. In doing so, we must weigh the interest the employer seeks to protect against the impact the covenant will have on the employee.

The provision in this contract should be upheld. The time limit is appropriate, restraining Strom from appearing on air for six months, during which time he will not appear on WCAP-TV in any case. It permits Strom to appear on air after a transition period tailored to allow Knox to develop an alternative broadcasting identity.

The geographical scope is appropriate, applying only to that broadcast area surrounding Columbia City. The provision restricts Strom's activity in the same media market as that in which his former employer operates.

The scope of the services covered is appropriate; the contract prohibits Strom from using an on-air personality in which Knox has a legitimate and protectable interest. Strom remains free to work for WCAP-TV as an off-air consultant.

Finally, enforcing the covenant in Strom's contract with Knox represents a fair balance of a distinct and substantial harm to Knox, when compared to a relatively minor and incidental harm to Strom.

We affirm.

Fawcett Railway Relief, Inc. v. Columbia Rail Services, Inc.

Columbia Court of Appeal (2015)

Fawcett Railway Relief, Inc. ("Fawcett") appeals from a declaratory judgment that voided a noncompetition covenant with Peter Markham ("Markham"), a former employee, and his new employer, Columbia Rail Services, Inc. ("CRS").

Fawcett is in the business of providing emergency disaster remediation services for railroads and industries with rail siding and rail yards in the lower 48 states, Canada, and Mexico. Markham began work for Fawcett in 2006 in Illinois, and over the course of seven years provided services in parts of Tennessee and Kentucky before locating in Columbia and performing services entirely within this state.

On December 2, 2011, after the move to Columbia, Markham entered into a renewed employment agreement with Fawcett that contained a non-compete provision. The non-compete provision prohibited Markham from working for three years in all of Florida, Columbia, Illinois, Ohio, Georgia, Kentucky, or Tennessee in any capacity.

On June 1, 2013, Markham left Fawcett and went to work for CRS, a direct competitor. Markham has worked for CRS only in Columbia. On April 7, 2014, CRS instituted this declaratory judgment action against Fawcett to have the covenant voided. The trial court agreed with CRS that the covenant involved was overly broad as to geographical scope, time period, and scope of services. It invalidated the covenant. Fawcett appealed.

The parties agree that Markham was an employee under this statute regulating covenants not to compete, Columbia Stat. Ann. § 24-6-53(a), and thus that the statute applied to this contract.

Fawcett contends that the trial court erred in invalidating the restrictive covenants as to their geographic scope, the scope of the services prohibited, and the time period of the restriction. For the reasons that follow, we disagree.

Geographic Scope

This geographic scope far exceeds the area within which Markham worked for Fawcett. This Court will accept as prima facie valid a restriction that covers the territory where the employee worked and the employer does business. However, a restriction that extends that territory to areas in which the employee did not work is overly broad on its face, absent a strong justification other than the desire not to compete with the former employee.

This restrictive covenant prohibited Markham from providing competing services in Florida, Columbia, Illinois, Ohio, Georgia, Kentucky, or Tennessee. The trial court's finding of fact noted that no east-west or north-south mainline railroad east of the Mississippi could operate without passing through this territory. Markham did not perform work in the entire eastern seaboard and in fact, performed work only in a limited area of some of the states listed in the restrictive covenant.

A restriction that covers a geographic area in which the employee never had contact with customers is overbroad and unreasonable. This covenant is unreasonably broad because it covers a region and areas of states where the plaintiff never worked.

Scope of Activity

The restrictive covenant in this case prevented Markham from performing work for any competitors of Fawcett both in the provision of emergency remediation services and "in any other capacity whatsoever."

Under our cases, a former employer may validly restrict an employee from performing services for a competitor that are identical to those performed for the former employer. Our courts have approved as reasonable restrictions that specifically state those activities related to the employer's business in which the employee was trained by the employer or worked for the employer. Such a restriction protects the employer's interests from competition in that area of service.

By contrast, a restrictive covenant that prohibits work for a competitor "in any capacity" does not protect a legitimate interest of the employer and imposes a greater limitation on the employee than is necessary. In this case, the contract prohibits Markham from working for a competitor in any capacity, including activities that have nothing to do with the services that he performed for Fawcett. This provision is unreasonably broad.

Duration of Restriction

The restrictive covenants in this case restricted Markham from competitive activity for a period of three years after the termination of his employment with Fawcett.

Our cases do not state a specific time period past which a given time restriction is per se unreasonable. Instead, the cases require employers who seek to uphold a time restriction to demonstrate how the restriction is necessary to the protection of the employer during the employee's transition to work for a competitor. An employer must prove specific facts and circumstances that support a finding of necessity. Absent such proof, our courts have invalidated time periods as short as one year or less.

The trial court in this case found that Fawcett offered no proof of the relationship between the time restriction and Fawcett's need for protection from competition. Moreover, we note that in none of our cases have we or our sister courts approved restrictions of longer than two years. We see no error in the trial court's conclusion that the three-year restriction in this case was unreasonable.

"Blue Pencilling"

Fawcett argues that the trial court erred in failing to "blue pencil" this covenant by modifying it to a more reasonable form, consistent with the situation and intentions of the parties. Fawcett argues that the court should have modified the provisions as follows: to restrict them to territories in which Markham had worked; to cover only the services that Markham had provided; and to be limited to the maximum time period approved by our prior cases (two years).

We disagree. The facts indicate that the covenants in this case bore no relationship to Fawcett's need for protection from competitive practices after Markham left its employ. This covenant not to compete is invalid and should not be revised. In such a situation, a trial court does not err in refusing to "blue pencil" the contract.

For all of the foregoing reasons, we affirm.

July 2021 California General Bar Examination Performance Test

II. Concise Outline for the Performance Test, July 2021

1. Statutory Mandate for Covenant Validity (Stat. Ann. § 24-6-53(a))

Rule: A covenant not to compete is only upheld if it is strictly limited and reasonable in time, geographic area, and scope of prohibited activities (Strom v. Knox Broadcasting Corp.).

Weighing Test: The court must weigh the employer's protectable interest against the covenant's impact (hardship) on the employee (Strom).

2. Geographic Scope (The Strongest Argument for Invalidity)

The Restriction: The covenant is for "anywhere in the State of Columbia."

Rule: A restriction is prima facie valid only if it covers the territory where the employee worked and the employer does business (Fawcett Railway Relief, Inc. v. Columbia Rail Services, Inc.).

Argument (Morgan): Morgan worked almost exclusively in Columbia City (northwest corner of the state), with only two outlying jobs. The statewide restriction is drastically overbroad and covers large regions (south/southeast) where Morgan never had contact with customers (Fawcett).

Conclusion: The geographic scope bears no relationship to Industrial's legitimate need for protection and must be invalidated.

3. Duration of Restriction (Time)

The Restriction: The covenant is for one (1) year.

Rule: The employer must prove the restriction is necessary for a transition period during the employee's departure (Fawcett).

Argument (Morgan): Industrial cannot demonstrate necessity.

Morgan testified that Industrial hired a replacement foreman the week before he left.

The existing bid manager "knew pretty much what [Morgan] knew," minimizing the expertise gap.

Counter/Rebuttal: Cole's claim of lost bids is not the "proof of specific facts and circumstances" necessary to uphold the duration (Fawcett).

4. Scope of Prohibited Activities and Protectable Interest

The Restriction: Prohibits working at any business in "sandblasting or similar industrial cleaning services."

Rule: The scope must be limited to activities identical to those performed for the employer and must protect a legitimate interest (e.g., substantial investment in an identity or specialized training) (Strom; Fawcett).

Argument (Morgan): Industrial is trying to protect Morgan's general professional expertise (sandblasting and bidding), which is not a protectable interest.

> **Industrial's investment is minimal**: Morgan claims he paid for the QP certifications himself, and the work experience is not comparable to the $1 million investment in an on-air persona upheld in Strom.
>
> The restriction, by attempting to cover general industry work, is overly broad, similar to the "in any capacity whatsoever" clause struck down in Fawcett.

5. Relief: Refusal to "Blue Pencil"

Rule: A court should refuse to modify (blue pencil) an invalid covenant if the covenants bore no relationship to the employer's need for protection (Fawcett).

Argument (Morgan): The covenant is invalid on all three prongs. The geographic scope (statewide) is so punitive and overreaching compared to Morgan's limited work area (Columbia City) that the entire provision must be voided, and the court should reject Industrial's request for the lesser remedy of restriction in Columbia City.

Hardship: Morgan will suffer severe financial harm (no work at all) if the covenant is enforced, tipping the balance in his favor (Strom).

July 2021 California General Bar Examination Performance Test

III. Comprehensive Guide for the Performance Test, July 2021

Initial Read Through

Audience and Format: The audience is the Judge (bench trial), and the format is an Oral Argument. This requires a confident, clear, and persuasive tone. Unlike an objective memo, you must select and present only the facts and legal interpretations that favor your client, Samuel Morgan.

Goal: The singular goal is to persuade the court to invalidate the entire covenant not to compete because it is unreasonably broad and imposes an unnecessary hardship on Morgan.

Core Statute: The entire analysis hinges on Columbia Stat. Ann. § 24-6-53(a), which requires the covenant to be reasonable in time, geographic area, and scope of prohibited activities.

Precise Issue Spotting

1. **Unreasonable Geographic Scope**: Whether the covenant's statewide restriction is unreasonably broad when Morgan's work was confined to a limited area.

2. **Unreasonable Duration/Lack of Necessity**: Whether Industrial has met its burden of proving the one-year duration is necessary to protect a legitimate interest when Morgan's replacement and knowledge base are already covered.

3. **Unreasonable Scope of Activity/Lack of Protectable Interest**: Whether the covenant seeks to protect Morgan's general professional expertise, which is not a legitimate employer interest, as opposed to specialized training or client relationships.

4. **Remedy**: Whether the court should refuse to "blue pencil" the invalid covenant, given its gross overbreadth.

Key Facts

1. **Geographic Scope**

Pro-Morgan Fact: Emphasize that Morgan worked almost exclusively in Columbia City, a limited area in the northwest corner of the state.

Countering Industrial: Argue that the statewide restriction is unreasonable because it covers large regions (South/Southeast) where Morgan never had customer contact (Fawcett).

2. Duration (Time)

Pro-Morgan Fact: Highlight that Industrial hired a replacement foreman the week before Morgan left, and the existing bid manager already "knew pretty much what [Morgan] knew."

Countering Industrial: Argue that Industrial's claim of lost bids is not proof of specific facts and circumstances supporting necessity for a full year (Fawcett).

3. Scope of Activity & Protectable Interest

Pro-Morgan Fact: Morgan paid for the QP certifications himself; Industrial's investment was minimal (only released him from work hours).

Countering Industrial: This level of investment is not the type of substantial investment or public persona that constitutes a protectable interest under Strom.

4. Hardship to Morgan

Pro-Morgan Fact: Stress that enforcing the covenant will result in Morgan having no work at all after years of experience.

Weighing: The court must weigh this severe hardship against Industrial's minimal interest (Strom).

Structuring the Answer

Introduction:

Identify yourself (Counsel for Defendant, Samuel Morgan).

State the core request (The covenant is invalid and unenforceable).

Briefly state the three reasons why (Unreasonable geographic scope, lack of necessity, no protectable interest).

Body/Arguments (The Reasonableness Test): Argue the three prongs using a modified IRAC approach, prioritizing the strongest argument first.

Argument 1: Geographic Scope (Strongest): Prove the statewide restriction is invalid using Fawcett.

Argument 2: Duration (Lack of Necessity): Prove the one-year term is unnecessary using Morgan's testimony about his replacements (Fawcett).

Argument 3: Scope & Protectable Interest (Minimal Investment): Prove Industrial's "investment" is minimal and doesn't meet the Strom standard.

Conclusion & Relief:

Summarize the failures of the covenant on all three prongs.

Address the "blue penciling" issue: Argue that the covenant is so grossly overbroad (especially geographically) that the court must refuse to modify it, as done in Fawcett.

Request relief: Deny the injunction and declare the covenant void.

Step by Step Process

Step 1: Attack Geographic Scope

Rule: A restriction is prima facie invalid if it exceeds the territory where the employee worked (Fawcett).

Application: Morgan worked exclusively in Columbia City (NW corner). The statewide restriction is a punitive and gross overreach.

Conclusion: This provision alone is so unreasonable it violates the statute and shows the covenant bears no relationship to Industrial's legitimate needs.

Step 2: Attack Duration (Lack of Necessity)

Rule: The employer must prove specific facts showing the duration is necessary for a transition period (Fawcett).

Application: Industrial cannot prove necessity. They already had a replacement foreman hired and an existing bid manager with the same knowledge. The purpose of a transition period (to mitigate harm) is already served.

Mitigation: Industrial's claim of lost bids is not the "proof of specific facts" needed to justify the restriction (Fawcett). The one-year term is unnecessary.

Step 3: Attack Scope of Activity (Lack of Protectable Interest)

Rule: The scope must protect a legitimate interest, such as a substantial investment in an employee's persona or highly specialized, company-specific training (Strom).

Application: Morgan paid for his own certifications. This is not the type of substantial investment that gives the employer a protectable interest, distinguishing it from the $1 million investment in the personality in Strom. Industrial is merely trying to restrict Morgan's general professional expertise, which is invalid (Fawcett).

Step 4: Address Blue Penciling and Hardship

Rule: If a covenant bears no relationship to the employer's need for protection, the court should refuse to modify it (Fawcett).

Application: Because the covenant fails on all three prongs—particularly the gross geographic overreach—the court should refuse Industrial's plea to enforce a lesser restriction (Columbia City only).

Weighing: Enforcement will cause Morgan severe financial harm (no work), tipping the required statutory balance decisively in favor of the employee (Strom).

Performance Test July 2021 (Employment Contracts: Covenants Not to Compete)

IV. Ultra Concise Answer, Performance Test, July 2021

DRAFT ORAL ARGUMENT

May it please the Court, my name is Applicant, and I represent the Defendant, Samuel Morgan. We respectfully request that this Court deny the plaintiff's motion for an injunction and declare the employment covenant void as unreasonable under Columbia Stat. Ann. § 24-6-53(a). This covenant fails the statutory test on all three required prongs: geographic scope, duration, and scope of prohibited activity.

First, the covenant's statewide geographic scope is grossly overbroad. Mr. Morgan testified he worked almost exclusively in Columbia City. As Fawcett Railway Relief holds, a restriction must be limited to the territory where the employee worked. A statewide ban, covering vast areas where Morgan never had customer contact, bears no relationship to Industrial's legitimate needs and is invalid ab initio.

Second, Industrial has failed to prove a protectable interest. The covenant attempts to restrict general industrial expertise. Industrial's investment was minimal; Mr. Morgan testified he paid for his own certifications. This is not the type of substantial investment in a unique persona or specialized training that Strom v. Knox requires.

Finally, the one-year duration is unnecessary. The employer must prove specific facts to justify the duration (Fawcett). Industrial cannot meet this burden, as they hired a replacement foreman the week before Morgan left, and the existing bid manager was already knowledgeable. Furthermore, enforcing this covenant will cause Mr. Morgan severe financial hardship—he will have no work at all—tipping the statutory balancing test decisively in his favor.

Because the covenant is grossly overbroad, particularly geographically, we urge the Court to follow Fawcett and refuse to "blue pencil" the provision. We request that the **entire covenant be declared void. Thank you, Your Honor**.

February 2021

California
Bar
Examination

Performance Test

INSTRUCTIONS AND FILE

MATTER OF I.B.I.

Instructions ....

FILE

Memorandum from Sarah Hodgeson to Applicant ....

Memorandum from Sarah Hodgeson to File:
Notes of Interview with Frank Duquesne ....

Article from Columbia Business Incubator Newsletter ....

Draft I.B.I. Contract Between Incubator and Mentor ....

Hodgeson and Hawkins, LLC
53 Severance Ridge Road
Columbia City, Columbia

MEMORANDUM

To: Applicant
From: Sarah Hodgeson
Date: February 23, 2021
Re: Matter of I.B.I.

Our firm represents Innovative Business Incubators (I.B.I.), a non-profit business that provides advice and support to new entrepreneurs in Columbia City. I.B.I. offers a range of services to new startups, including advice, expert consulting, networking, and referrals to other professional services. I recently met with Frank Duquesne, the Executive Director of I.B.I.

One of I.B.I.'s main services is the arranging of mentoring relationship between new entrepreneurs and experienced mentors. As the attached interview notes and article explain, these mentors can provide value that I.B.I. cannot, including expertise tailored to the needs of particular kinds of business.

Recently, after a complaint about a mentor, Duquesne has decided that he needs to formalize the relationship between I.B.I. and its mentors. He provided me with an article that highlights the benefits and the risks of the mentoring relationship in an incubator context. He has also provided me with a draft contract that he has revised to include the basic parameters that he wants to set on the relationship.

I want you to write a memo assessing several legal issues arising out of the relationship between mentor and mentee. For each of the following questions, I want you to assess the impact of the law on the draft contract and, without drafting new language, describe any changes you might recommend to address our client's concerns:

1. Whether the relationship between an I.B.I. mentor and mentee gives rise to fiduciary obligations owed by the mentor to the mentee;

2. Whether the draft contract between I.B.I. and a mentor creates contractual rights that an I.B.I. mentee can assert against the mentor.

Hodgeson and Hawkins, LLC
53 Severance Ridge Road
Columbia City, Columbia

MEMORANDUM

To: File

From: Sarah Hodgeson

Date: February 21, 2021

Re: Matter of I.B.I.: Initial Interview with Frank Duquesne

I met with Frank Duquesne today. He's the Executive Director of Innovative Business Incubators (I.B.I.), a private non-profit that helps startup businesses with services and advice. Frank is an old acquaintance who, after several years working in business, started I.B.I. as a way of providing help to new entrepreneurs.

Frank told me that, for several years after starting I.B.I., he and his paid staff provided almost all of the support services to mentees: help with business basics; networking activities; internet access; advice on finding loans, managing accounts, and developing businesses.

Eventually, Frank told me, he realized that his mentees would benefit from working directly with established business people in areas where I.B.I. lacked expertise. He created several informal mentoring relationships between these "mentors" and his mentees. These relationships worked well, so he decided to make mentoring a regular and important part of I.B.I.'s service.

He recruited a team of over 30 mentors, all located in the capital city, representing a diversity of business structures and business types. I.B.I. now routinely offers to connect its mentees with mentors and Frank is aggressively seeking out new mentors for business models and services with which he is not familiar.

Recently, however, Frank received a complaint from one of his startup mentees. The mentee reported that one of I.B.I.'s mentors had pressured the mentee to use the mentor's business as a principal supplier, on terms less favorable than the mentee could obtain elsewhere. Moreover, this same mentor had also pressured the mentee to allow him to invest in the business, in exchange for a significant ownership share. The mentee resisted both advances and ended the relationship.

Frank stressed that this kind of problem had only occurred once. He believes that, in most circumstances, both mentor and mentee will act in good faith, that the mentees will seek independent advice before transacting with a mentor, and that strong reasons can exist for such transactions, involving benefits for both parties.

However, Frank wants to clarify the relationships between I.B.I., its mentors, and its mentees. He did some research and found some model mentoring agreements that he revised and proposes to ask his mentors to sign. He proposes to use such an agreement with all of his mentors. Before he does so, he wants us to review the agreements and advise him about the legal consequences for I.B.I.'s mentors.

Before our meeting ended, I spent time exploring what goals he wanted these agreements to serve. As I expected, Frank identified several conflicting concerns:

- Protecting I.B.I.'s Startup Mentees: Given the feedback from this one mentee, Frank wants to make sure that both he and his mentees have a way to protect the mentee legally if a mentor does succeed in taking advantage of the mentee.

- Avoiding the Discouragement of Mentors: At the same time, Frank does not want to expose his mentors to unnecessary liability. In most cases, mentors volunteer their time. He doesn't want the threat of lawsuits to chill that willingness to help.

- Informality: Frank is more than willing to ask mentors to contract with I.B.I., but he wants to preserve the informality and open-endedness of the relationships between mentors and mentee/mentees. He strongly believes that these relationships work best if mentors and mentees work in good faith, without asking them to sign binding contracts defining the relationship.

I told Frank that we would research his questions and get back to him soon.

Business Incubators and Business Mentors: Helpful or Harmful?

Columbia Business Incubator Newsletter

A business incubator helps startup companies to grow by providing services such as management training or office space. Business incubators differ from industrial parks in their dedication to startup and early-stage companies. Incubators also differ from the Small Business Development Centers (and similar government sponsored business support programs) in that they serve only selected clients.

The formal concept of business incubation began in the USA in 1959 when Joseph Mancuso opened the Batavia Industrial Center in a Batavia, New York, warehouse. Since then, incubators have spread across the globe; by some estimates, as many as 7,000 business incubators exist world-wide.

Technology has increased this growth. New experiments like Virtual Business Incubators bring the resources of entrepreneurship hubs like Silicon Valley to remote locations all over the world. Virtual incubators allow startups to get the benefit of an incubator without actually being located at the incubator site.

Many incubators rely on business mentors to help as advisors and consultants for startup businesses. These mentors typically come from the same industry as the startup and include established individuals with substantial business experience.

A good mentor can be a huge plus. Mentors bring knowledge and perspective that allow startups to avoid hidden risks and to seize unseen opportunities. A mentor can provide entry into specialized business networks and can help new business people form relationships with suppliers, customers, and regulators.

At the same time, the mentoring relationship can have its downsides. Mentors sometimes take too little time to learn the new business. Mentors may fail to understand new or disruptive business models. Finally, some mentors have used their position of influence to take an ownership position in the startup or to sign contracts that benefit the mentor's own business.

Before using the services of an incubator or a business mentor, take time to understand how the incubator and the mentor work. Ask for copies of the mentoring agreement. If you do work with a mentor, make sure to seek a second opinion before entering into an investment or contractual relationship with your mentor.

AGREEMENT WITH BUSINESS MENTORS

This Agreement is between Innovative Business Incubator (I.B.I.), a non-profit in the State of Columbia, and ____________________, an individual (Mentor), desiring to provide business and professional guidance to individuals and businesses using the services of I.B.I. (Mentee(s)).

With this Agreement, I.B.I. and the Mentor seek to accomplish the following goals:

— to protect the respective interests of I.B.I., the Mentor, and the Mentees;

— to clarify the relationships between I.B.I., the Mentor, and the Mentees; and

— to ensure the confidentiality of information disclosed in the context of counseling or technical assistance.

Accordingly, I.B.I. and the Mentor agree as follows:

1. <u>The Mentor agrees</u>:

   a) Not to charge a fee or accept a gift (or secure same or another) for counseling or other services provided to the Mentee;

   b) Not to service competing Mentees at the same time prior to notifying all competing Mentees that the Mentor is providing services to competing Mentees;

   c) Not to discuss Mentee information or the counseling relationship with anyone other than I.B.I. personnel; and

   d) Not to withdraw from a counseling assignment without first notifying I.B.I.

2. <u>Duration</u>: The Mentor agrees that this Agreement shall remain in force and in effect, from the date hereof, during the term of its relationship with any Mentee.

3. Remedies: In the event of any breach of this Agreement, I.B.I. is entitled to enforce the terms of this Agreement through actions that may include actions for damages or injunctive relief or other remedies.

IN WITNESS WHEREOF, the undersigned parties have duly executed this Agreement.

I.B.I.	MENTOR:
______________________________	______________________________
(name) (title)	(name) (title)
Date:	Date:

February 2021

California
Bar
Examination

Performance Test
LIBRARY

MATTER OF I.B.I.

LIBRARY

Togs for Tots, Inc. v. CCM
Columbia Supreme Court (2011) ....

Norton v. Kramer
Columbia Supreme Court (2007) ....

Togs for Tots, Inc. v. CCM

Columbia Supreme Court (2011)

Jeremy Painter owns Togs for Tots, Inc., a Columbia corporation that markets children's clothing to retailers. Children's Clothing Manufacturer, or "CCM," manufactures children's clothing in Columbia.

In 2001, Painter approached Ronald Denito, owner of CCM, with a business proposition: Denito should create a company to manufacture children's clothing that Painter would then sell. As a result, Denito started up CCM. Painter and Denito agreed that CCM would manufacture products, that Painter would market those products to the retail trade, and that Painter would act as CCM's sole marketer.

Through his company, Togs for Tots, Painter then began to create a market for the products CCM manufactured and sold under its name. Togs for Tots paid all costs of the sales effort, including travel expenses and the maintenance of a showroom office in Columbia. Painter held himself out to the retail trade as a partner in CCM and carried a business card designating him as Vice President of CCM. From 2002 to 2008, Togs for Tots solely engaged in marketing products for CCM.

During this time, Painter and Denito made all business decisions together. CCM handled the manufacturing aspect, while Togs for Tots handled the marketing. At trial, Painter alleges that he and Denito shared "a confidential relationship." Painter and Denito shared the profits of CCM, with Painter receiving marketing profits in the form of commissions and Denito receiving manufacturing profit.

As a result of Painter's marketing efforts, by 2009, CCM grossed $15 million in annual sales. This included $12 million from Walmart, CCM's biggest customer. To obtain Walmart as a client, Painter helped design a unique line of clothes that CCM manufactured exclusively for sale under Walmart's private label.

In October 2009, CCM terminated their relationship with Togs for Tots. At that time, Denito informed Painter that defendants could no longer afford to share their revenues with plaintiffs.

Painter and Togs for Tots then filed suit, claiming that both Denito and CCM had breached a contract and, separately, that Denito and CCM had breached a duty arising out of a confidential relationship. Defendants moved to dismiss all claims. The trial court dismissed the claim as to breach of contract, but did not dismiss the confidential relationship claim. The defendants appealed this decision; the Columbia Court of Appeals affirmed.

In this appeal, CCM contends that Painter and Togs for Tots have failed to establish the existence of a confidential relationship between them, and that this cause of action must also be dismissed.

To succeed on a claim for breach of fiduciary duty in Columbia, a plaintiff must prove three elements: (1) a fiduciary duty between the parties; (2) defendant's breach of that duty; and (3) damages that were proximately caused by the breach. If proven, such a claim can result in liability independent of any contract between the parties.

The first element requires proof of the existence of a fiduciary duty. In some cases, such a duty arises out of a relationship well recognized as such: agent and principal; trustee and beneficiary; or guardian and ward. In other cases, the duties may arise out of relationships outside the standard fiduciary models. In such cases, the plaintiff must prove the existence of a "confidential relationship" as a matter of fact.

The existence of a confidential relationship cannot be determined by recourse to rigid formulas. A confidential relationship may exist where one person relies on another because of a history of trust, older age, family connection, and/or superior training and knowledge, and where the person relied upon assumes a position of dominance in the relationship. Reliance and dominance are the key factors in such a relationship. In the relationship between a business advisor and client, the advisor may bring more knowledge, expertise, or financial resources than the advisee. The resulting inequality could impose duties on the advisor to refrain from self-dealing or from exacting inequitable terms.

For example, in *Shaw v. Benedetti Enterprises* (2007), defendant Benedetti hired Shaw as an advisor to help Benedetti create a business that would manufacture and market durable medical equipment. Shaw sued for unpaid commissions, and Benedetti counterclaimed for breach of a confidential relationship. On the facts of that case, we found no such relationship. The parties had entered into a bargained-for exchange, pursuant to which each party received some benefit. We refused to extend duties of a confidential relationship to everyday commercial activity. To do so would expose participants to unexpected liability and could erode the exacting standards applied to those in a true fiduciary relationship with each other.

In this case, the pleadings do not indicate that either Painter or Denito had substantially greater knowledge, expertise, or financial resources than the other. In fact, Painter initiated the relationship and provided his share of the capital required to start up the marketing relationship. Moreover, the pleadings indicate a history of bargained-for collaboration resulting in substantial profits for both parties.

The trial court erred in failing to dismiss the plaintiffs' claim based on an alleged confidential relationship.

Accordingly, we reverse.

Norton v. Kramer

Columbia Supreme Court (2007)

This case arises from a lawsuit filed by Josephine Norton and several others against Samuel Kramer. Norton and her co-plaintiffs claim to be third-party beneficiaries of a contract between Kramer, acting under the name of Joseph Morgan, and the Columbia Basin Retreat (Retreat). The plaintiffs alleged that Kramer breached this contract by concealing his identity and by fraudulently inducing the plaintiffs to reside at the Retreat for over ten years.

Samuel Kramer formed the Retreat in 1992 as a non-profit corporation. He appointed himself as the spiritual leader of the Retreat, using the name of Joseph Morgan. In so doing, Kramer concealed his background as a former art student at the Columbia College of Art and as a failed retail merchant.

The Retreat included approximately twenty resident members (Residents) and operated a small public center for teaching yoga. In 1995, the Retreat moved to a 150-acre site in Lenox County, Columbia, which contained several large facilities. Between 1995 and 2006, over 8,000 paying guests per year visited the Retreat "to relax, take yoga classes, meditate, have massages, and otherwise take a break from the routine of their daily lives." The Residents operated the facility, working for room and board and a small monthly stipend in exchange for the opportunity to live at the Retreat as Morgan's "disciples."

The Residents allege that they, the paying guests, and donors were attracted to the facility precisely because of Morgan's presence. Morgan's picture hung throughout the facilities, his videos ran continuously in the public areas, and his books, tapes, and other items were offered for sale by the Retreat. Publicly, Morgan claimed to be an authentic teacher and object of veneration, one who attained his status through several forms of abstinence. Morgan outwardly professed "honesty, selfless devotion to the well-being of his followers," and "absolute personal trust" between teacher and disciples, as well as celibacy and a physically and financially simple lifestyle.

The Residents characterize Morgan as cultivating an intense emotional dependence on him. They were told to identify themselves and their well-being with Morgan and to regard him as the most important person in their lives. He frequently offered guidance on the most intimate aspects of the Residents' personal lives. They state that, over many years, each of them developed a "close and deeply personal relationship" with Morgan. They state that they endeavored to be chaste, honest, selfless, and devoted to the well-being of others. At Morgan's urging, many donated all of their possessions to the Retreat, in some cases as much as $100,000.

The Residents claim that, in fact, Morgan/Kramer was a fraud. Their complaint alleges that, from 1992 through 2005, the Retreat entered into a series of lucrative contractual relationships with Kramer, to induce him to remain physically present at the Retreat. Kramer received an annual fee, free housing, free transportation (both domestic and international), a percentage of the proceeds from literature, video, and audiotape sales, and free sponsorship of seminars throughout the world. He retained the revenue from these operations in an amount of many hundreds of thousands of dollars.

Kramer left the Retreat after the discovery of his background by an author hired to write his authorized biography. The Residents brought this lawsuit, claiming intentional infliction of emotional distress; breach of fiduciary duty; breach of contract on a third party beneficiary theory of recovery; fraud and misrepresentation; and unfair and deceptive trade practices.

Kramer moved to dismiss all claims. The trial court dismissed all but the fiduciary duty, fraud, and trade practices complaints. The Residents appealed the dismissal of their breach of contract claims to the Court of Appeals, which affirmed the dismissal. We also affirm.

The Residents' complaint alleges that the Retreat contracted with Kramer for his services and that they, as resident members of the Retreat, were the intended beneficiaries of such contracts. According to them, Kramer breached these contracts when he misrepresented his status as a "true and authentic teacher" for the purpose of amassing significant personal wealth.

To recover as third-party beneficiaries, the Residents must show that they were intended beneficiaries of a contract between the defendant and the Retreat. Only intended beneficiaries, not incidental beneficiaries, can enforce a contract. A party is an intended beneficiary if performance under the contract effectuates the intention of the parties, and if circumstances indicate that the beneficiary would receive the benefit of the promised performance. See Restatement (Second) of Contracts § 302(1)(b).

The key question is the intent of the parties to the actual contract to confer a benefit on a third party. That intent must appear from the contract itself or be shown by necessary implication. For example, if A and B enter into a contract whereby A agrees to pay B to construct a house for C, it is clear that C is an intended beneficiary. Similarly, if X and Y enter into a contract whereby Y will provide a service to C, C has the right to enforce the terms of that contract against Y.

The Residents allege that Kramer, for valuable consideration, contracted with the Retreat to provide services to the customers and Residents of the Retreat. Construed in a light favorable to the Residents, the terms of those contracts required Kramer to remain physically present at the Retreat, teach yoga courses, meet with guests and visitors, and serve as advisor, mentor and exemplar to the Residents, in addition to providing counseling services to his followers.

These allegations, if proven, would be sufficient to conclude that the Residents were intended beneficiaries of his agreement with the Retreat. They may maintain an action for breach of contract as third-party beneficiaries. However, this conclusion does not end the discussion; the facts as alleged by the plaintiffs simply fail to state a claim for breach of the contract between Kramer and the Retreat.

The gist of the Residents' complaint is that, by secretly reaping substantial monetary compensation, Kramer was not providing the services of an "authentic" teacher. The required services included the development of a close mentoring relationship with the plaintiffs, as an exemplar of a particular lifestyle. But plaintiffs' own complaint indicates that Kramer satisfied those requirements: "Over many years, each of the plaintiffs developed a close and deeply personal relationship with Kramer."

To achieve the result sought by the Residents, the contract would have had to limit the financial benefits to Kramer or to require him either to act or refrain from acting in ways that complied with particular standards of behavior. But nothing in the complaint indicates that the contract specifically required Kramer to adhere to a particular code of conduct or abjure any specific behavior to maintain his status. Considering the liberal financial benefits obtained by Kramer, it is difficult to conclude that the contract intended such terms. Even taking all the Residents' allegations as true, Kramer's conduct does not constitute a breach of any specific terms of the contract between him and the Retreat.

In sum, although the Residents are third-party beneficiaries of the contract between the Retreat and Kramer, nothing in their complaint states a claim for breach of contract. Accordingly, we affirm the dismissal of this count of their complaint. We note that their claims for breach of fiduciary duty, for fraud, and for unfair and deceptive trade practices were not dismissed and are not affected by our decision. Plaintiffs may pursue those claims at trial.

Affirmed.

Performance Test Feb 2021 (Contracts Fiduciary Duty & Third-Party Beneficiary)

II. Concise Outline for the Performance Test, February 2021

1. Fiduciary Obligations Owed by Mentor to Mentee

Core Issue: Whether the informality and superior expertise of the mentor create a "confidential relationship" giving rise to fiduciary duties, particularly concerning self-dealing and inequitable terms (Togs for Tots, Inc. v. CCM).

Argument for Fiduciary Duty (Mentee's Side):

Reliance and Dominance (Key Factors): The mentor provides "expert consulting" and "specialized business networks," creating inequality due to superior knowledge and resources (Togs for Tots).

Unequal Position: The mentor is in a position of influence, which led to a clear example of self-dealing (pressuring mentee to use mentor's supplier/investing for ownership share).

Argument Against Fiduciary Duty (Mentor/I.B.I. Side):

Informality: Frank Duquesne's goal is to preserve the "informality and open-endedness" of the relationship, avoiding formal liability.

Commercial Activity: The relationship involves a "bargained-for exchange" of guidance for startup success. Togs for Tots warns against extending confidential duties to "everyday commercial activity" to avoid unexpected liability.

Mentee Advice: The Article advises mentees to "seek a second opinion" before entering contracts with a mentor, suggesting an arms-length commercial relationship, not a fully trusted fiduciary one.

Conclusion: The facts strongly suggest a confidential relationship could be proven due to reliance and dominance, which poses a serious liability risk to I.B.I.'s mentors.

2. Contractual Rights Asserted by Mentee Against Mentor

Core Issue: Whether the draft contract's stated goal to "protect the respective interests... of the Mentees" establishes the mentees as intended third-party beneficiaries with enforceable rights (Norton v. Kramer).

Argument for Third-Party Beneficiary Status (Mentee's Side):

Intent to Benefit (Restatement § 302(1)(b)): The contract preamble explicitly states a goal is to "protect the respective interests... of the Mentees," indicating an intent to confer a benefit (Norton v. Kramer).

Service Analogy: The Mentor's agreement with I.B.I. is to provide a service (counseling/guidance) directly to the Mentee, establishing them as an intended beneficiary (analogous to Y providing service to C in Norton).

Argument Against Enforceability (Mentor/I.B.I. Side):

No Breach of Specific Term (The Norton Limit): Even if the mentee is an intended beneficiary, they cannot sue unless the mentor breached a specific term of the contract (Norton v. Kramer).

Remedies Clause: The contract explicitly grants the enforcement remedy only to I.B.I.: "I.B.I. is entitled to enforce the terms of this Agreement." This actively limits the mentee's power to sue.

Conclusion: Mentees are likely intended beneficiaries, but the current contract draft likely protects the mentors because only I.B.I. is granted the right to seek remedies for a breach.

Recommended Contract Changes (Based on Client's Conflicting Concerns)

To Protect Mentees (Client Goal #1): Add an explicit provision requiring the Mentor to acknowledge and waive conflicts of interest when dealing with Mentees.

To Avoid Discouraging Mentors / Preserve Informality (Client Goal #2 & #3): Add a provision clarifying that the contract does not create any third-party beneficiary rights for Mentees and that Mentors are independent, non-fiduciaries, subject only to enforcement by I.B.I.

Performance Test Feb 2021 (Contracts Fiduciary Duty & Third-Party Beneficiary)

III. Comprehensive Guide for the Performance Test, February 2021

Initial Read Through

Audience & Format: The audience is your supervising attorney, Sarah Hodgeson. The format is an Objective Memorandum. The memo must assess the legal issues and, critically, describe any changes you might recommend to the draft contract to address the client's concerns.

Assignment: The memo must answer two separate, specific legal questions in a neutral, objective tone.

Client Conflicts: Note Frank Duquesne's conflicting concerns, which must be addressed in your recommended changes:

Goal 1: Protecting Mentees (e.g., from self-dealing).

Goal 2 & 3: Avoiding Discouragement of Mentors / Preserving Informality.

Precise Issue Spotting

1. Fiduciary Obligations: Whether the relationship between an I.B.I. mentor and mentee gives rise to fiduciary obligations owed by the mentor to the mentee.

2. Contractual Rights: Whether the draft contract between I.B.I. and a mentor creates contractual rights that an I.B.I. mentee can assert against the mentor.

Key Facts

Issue 1 (Fiduciary Duty) Facts:

Mentor's Position: Provides "expert consulting" and expertise tailored to the business (superior knowledge/training).

Mentor's Influence: One mentor used their position to pressure a mentee into a self-dealing supply contract and seek a significant ownership share.

Client Goal: Client wants to preserve the informality of the relationships and avoid unnecessary liability for volunteer mentors.

Issue 2 (Third-Party Beneficiary) Facts:

Parties to Contract: The contract is exclusively between I.B.I. and the Mentor.

Preamble Intent: The contract goals explicitly state the intent "to protect the respective interests... of the Mentees."

Remedy Clause: The contract explicitly limits enforcement to I.B.I.: "I.B.I. is entitled to enforce the terms of this Agreement."

Structuring the Answer

CAPTION/HEADER: Include TO:, FROM:, DATE:, and RE:.

QUESTIONS PRESENTED: Rephrase the two Task Memo questions into neutral, formal legal issues.

BRIEF ANSWERS: Provide a short, direct answer (a single sentence or two) for each of the two questions.

DISCUSSION: This section houses the full IRAC analysis for each of the two issues. Use clear subheadings corresponding to the Questions Presented.

RECOMMENDATIONS: Provide specific recommendations based on your legal findings, tailored to address the client's conflicting goals.

Step by Step Process

Step 1: Analyze Fiduciary Duty (Issue 1)

Rule: Start with the rule that a duty may arise outside a standard fiduciary model if a "confidential relationship" is proven (Togs for Tots). The key factors are Reliance and Dominance.

Application Strategy (Arguing for Liability):

Mentors have superior knowledge/expertise, creating a resulting inequality (Dominance).

Mentees rely on this expertise for specialized advice (Reliance).

The single instance of self-dealing confirms the position of influence and the potential for abuse of the relationship, which Togs for Tots suggests can impose a duty to refrain from self-dealing.

Application Strategy (Arguing Against Liability):

The relationship is primarily a "bargained-for exchange" for business support, which Togs for Tots warns against extending fiduciary duties to, as it would expose mentors to unexpected liability.

The client's goal is to preserve informality.

Conclusion: Conclude that a confidential relationship is likely to be found due to the facts supporting dominance and reliance, posing a risk to the mentors.

Step 2: Analyze Third-Party Beneficiary Rights (Issue 2)

Rule: Only intended beneficiaries may enforce a contract (Restatement § 302(1)(b) via Norton v. Kramer). Intent must appear from the contract itself or by necessary implication.

Application Strategy (Intended Beneficiary Status):

The contract's preamble explicitly states the intent is "to protect the respective interests... of the Mentees," which clearly indicates an intent to confer a benefit (Norton).

The performance (guidance and counseling) is rendered directly to the Mentee, establishing them as an intended beneficiary.

Application Strategy (Enforceability Limitation):

Pivot immediately to the Norton v. Kramer limitation: Even as an intended beneficiary, a mentee cannot sue unless the mentor breached a specific term of the contract.

The current contract is very vague (e.g., "Not to charge a fee").

Crucially, the Remedies clause actively limits enforcement: "I.B.I. is entitled to enforce the terms..." This language strongly suggests the parties intended I.B.I. to be the sole party with the right to sue.

Conclusion: Conclude that the Mentees are likely intended beneficiaries, but the current contract prevents them from successfully enforcing its terms due to the Norton limitation and the specific Remedies clause.

Step 3: Recommendations (Addressing Conflicting Goals)

Protect Mentees (Goal 1): To address the self-dealing example, recommend adding a clause that requires the Mentor to disclose any potential conflict of interest or waive the right to enter into commercial transactions with the mentee.

Avoid Discouragement/Informality (Goals 2 & 3): To protect the mentor, recommend adding an explicit clause that:

Disclaims Fiduciary Duty: State that the relationship is non-fiduciary.

Disclaims Third-Party Rights: State that the contract does not create any third-party beneficiary rights for Mentees.

Performance Test Feb 2021 (Contracts Fiduciary Duty & Third-Party Beneficiary)

IV. Ultra Concise Answer, Performance Test, February 2021

TO: Sarah Hodgeson
FROM: Applicant
DATE: February 23, 2021
RE: Matter of I.B.I. – Mentor Liability Assessment

QUESTIONS PRESENTED

Whether a mentor's superior expertise and position of influence create a confidential relationship giving rise to fiduciary obligations toward an I.B.I. mentee.

Whether the draft contract creates enforceable contractual rights for a mentee as a third-party beneficiary against an I.B.I. mentor.

BRIEF ANSWERS

Yes. The facts supporting the mentor's dominance and the mentee's reliance make a finding of a confidential relationship likely, subjecting the mentor to fiduciary duties against self-dealing (Togs for Tots).

No. While mentees are likely intended beneficiaries, the contract explicitly limits the remedy to I.B.I., preventing a mentee from successfully asserting a claim for breach (Norton v. Kramer).

DISCUSSION

I. The Mentor-Mentee Relationship Risks Creating Fiduciary Obligations.

A fiduciary duty may arise from a confidential relationship defined by reliance and dominance (Togs for Tots). I.B.I. mentors provide "expert consulting" and superior knowledge, creating the inequality necessary to impose a duty to refrain from self-dealing.

The fact that one mentor pressured a mentee into a supply contract and sought ownership confirms the mentor's position of dominance. While I.B.I. seeks to maintain informality, this advisory role transcends everyday commercial activity (Togs for Tots), meaning the risk of fiduciary liability is high for mentors who engage in self-interested transactions with mentees.

II. The Contract Confers Intended Benefits but Prevents Mentee Enforcement.

Mentees are likely intended beneficiaries because the contract's preamble explicitly seeks "to protect the respective interests... of the Mentees," and the performance (counseling) is rendered directly to them (Norton v. Kramer).

However, intended beneficiary status alone is insufficient to enforce the contract. The contract's Remedies clause explicitly limits enforcement rights to I.B.I.: "I.B.I. is entitled to enforce the terms of this Agreement." Because the mentee is not granted the right to sue, they cannot maintain an action against the mentor for breach (Norton v. Kramer).

RECOMMENDED CONTRACT CHANGES

To balance I.B.I.'s conflicting goals (protecting mentees vs. protecting mentors):

Protect Mentees: Add a clause requiring Mentors to disclose any conflicts of interest and waive the right to enter into commercial transactions with a mentee for the duration of the relationship.

Protect Mentors: Add language explicitly stating that the contract does not create any third-party beneficiary rights for Mentees and that Mentors are acting as independent, non-fiduciary advisors.

October 2020

California
Bar
Examination

Performance Test
INSTRUCTIONS AND FILE

IN RE POTENTIAL WRIGHT LITIGATION

Instructions ....

FILE

Memorandum to Applicant from Margery Turner ....

Memorandum to File re Potential Wright Litigation ....

Letter re Unauthorized Charges ....

MEMORANDUM

To: **Applicant**
From: **Margery Turner**
Date: **October 6, 2020**
Re: **Potential Wright Litigation**

Janice Wright, a long-time client, has retained us on a matter concerning unauthorized credit card charges run up by her son, Ryan, for online purchases connected to an online video gaming website called GamerTrax. At Ryan's request, Janice gave him permission to open an account using her credit card. She told him he could charge no more than $20; he ended up charging $9,000. After receiving her credit card bill, she sent a letter to GamerTrax asking for a reversal of the $8,980 charge, but GamerTrax declined. She would like our help in determining whether she can avoid paying some or all of the charges.

I have already determined that Ryan was able to, and did in fact, enter into a contract with GamerTrax. So that I may discuss this matter with Janice, please prepare a memorandum that answers the following questions:

1 Is Ryan able to disaffirm the contract?
2. If so, did Janice's letter disaffirm the contract for Ryan?
3. Is Janice liable for the $8,980 charge?

Do not include a statement of facts in your memorandum, but do use the facts in its body.

MEMORANDUM

To: File

From: Margery Turner

Date: September 29, 2020

Re: Potential Wright Litigation

I met with long-time client Janice Wright yesterday to discuss a matter involving online video game activity by her 12-year-old son, Ryan.

The GamerTrax website allows users to play a wide array of online video games for free. Ryan, an avid online video gamer, has regularly done so.

The GamerTrax website also allows users to buy certain "options" to enhance their online video gaming experience. These options include "extra weapons," which can increase the user's chance of winning a game, and "extra lives," which can extend the duration of a game. To enable users to buy such options, the GamerTrax website maintains a payment system called GamerTrax Treasure.

Two months ago, at Ryan's request, Janice gave Ryan permission to open a GamerTrax Treasure account using her credit card. Janice gave Ryan the credit card number, expiration date, and security code, and told him that he could spend no more than $20.

Ryan opened a GamerTrax Treasure account. In doing so, he clicked, "I have read, understand, and agree to the Terms of Service," which included the following:

1. "I agree to provide a valid credit or debit card to obtain any option(s) for any online video game(s)."

2. "I agree that I am authorized to use the valid credit or debit card provided, either as the holder of the card if it is in my name or as an agent of the holder of the card if it is in the name of another. I further agree that I am authorized to use the valid credit or debit card provided in any and all amounts, up to and including the limit established by the issuer."

3. "I agree that all transactions I may enter into to obtain any option(s) for any online video game(s) are final and irreversible."

4. "I am under the age of eighteen (18), have reviewed the foregoing Terms of Service with my parent(s) or guardian(s), and have his/her/their permission to agree as stated above. To verify, you may contact my parent(s)/guardian(s) at jwright@columbiavalley.com."

GamerTrax contacted Janice and she verified that she had given Ryan permission.

After opening the GamerTrax Treasure account, Ryan started playing an online video game called Galactic Odyssey, and obtained a few options. Janice's credit card was charged $20. Ryan continued playing Galactic Odyssey for weeks, and obtained numerous additional options. He did not believe that he was spending any money to obtain these additional options. He was wrong: Janice's credit card was charged an additional $8,980.

When Janice received her credit card bill, she sent a letter to GamerTrax asking for a reversal of the $8,980 charge. GamerTrax declined.

Janice has not yet paid her credit card bill, pending consultation with us.

Ms. Janice Wright
234 Elm Street
Lincoln, Columbia

September 21, 2020

GamerTrax, Inc.
GamerTrax Campus
Moline Park, Columbia

Re: Unauthorized Charges

Dear Sir or Madam:

I am writing to request that you reverse the amount of $8,980 for unauthorized charges to my credit card. I authorized my son, Ryan Wright, to use my credit card to charge no more than $20 for options for online video games. I did not learn until I received my credit card bill that he had used it to charge an additional $8,980 for such options.

Thank you for your prompt attention to this matter.

Very truly yours,

Janice Wright

October 2020

California
Bar
Examination

Performance Test
LIBRARY

IN RE POTENTIAL WRIGHT LITIGATION

LIBRARY

Select Provisions of the Columbia Civil Code ....

Select Provisions of the Columbia Family Code ....

Miller v. Miller
Columbia Court of Appeal (1963) ....

Brady v. Thomas
Columbia Court of Appeal (2004) ....

Laredo v. Purcell Fruit Co.
Columbia Supreme Court (1950) ....

SELECT PROVISIONS OF THE COLUMBIA CIVIL CODE

Section 3800. Agency Defined.

Agency is the fiduciary relationship that arises when one person (a "principal") manifests assent to another person (an "agent") that the agent shall act on the principal's behalf and subject to the principal's control, and the agent manifests assent or otherwise consents so to act.

Section 3801. Actual Authority.

An agent acts with actual authority when, at the time of taking action that has legal consequences for the principal, the agent reasonably believes, in accordance with the principal's manifestations to the agent, that the principal wishes the agent so to act.

Section 3802. Apparent Authority.

Apparent authority is the power held by an agent or other actor to affect a principal's legal relations with third parties when a third party reasonably believes the actor has authority to act on behalf of the principal and that belief is traceable to the principal's manifestations.

Section 3803. Creation of Actual Authority.

Actual authority is created by a principal's manifestation to an agent that, as reasonably understood by the agent, expresses the principal's assent that the agent take action on the principal's behalf.

<u>Section 3804</u>. Creation of Apparent Authority.

Apparent authority is created by a person's manifestation that another has authority to act with legal consequences for the person who makes the manifestation, when a third party reasonably believes the actor to be authorized and the belief is traceable to the manifestation.

* * *

<u>Section 3810</u>. Binding Effect.

Any act of an agent within the scope of his or her actual or apparent authority binds the principal.

SELECT PROVISIONS OF THE COLUMBIA FAMILY CODE

Section 6701. Minor's Power to Contract.

A minor may make a contract in the same manner as an adult, subject to the power of disaffirmance under Section 6702.

Section 6702. Minor's Power to Disaffirm.

Except as provided in Section 6703, a contract of a minor may be disaffirmed by the minor or by the minor's parent or guardian before majority or within a reasonable time afterwards.

Section 6703. Exception to Minor's Power to Disaffirm.

A contract, otherwise valid, entered into during minority, may not be disaffirmed on that ground if: (a) the contract is to pay the reasonable value of things necessary for the support of the minor or the minor's family; (b) these things have been actually furnished to the minor or to the minor's family; and (c) the contract is entered into by the minor when not under the care of a parent or guardian able to provide for the minor or the minor's family.

Miller v. Miller

Columbia Court of Appeal (1963)

By his complaint, Bryce Miller sought judgment against his mother Josephine Miller for $26,000, representing payments issued to him when he was under 18 years of age under a contract of employment as an actor. Bryce now appeals from a judgment in favor of Josephine.

Bryce was born March 11, 1940. In 1953, Bryce entered into a contract with Couch Studios, Inc., to portray a role in a television series. At the same time, Bryce entered into a contract with Josephine, under which she relinquished any right to any money paid to him pursuant to his contract with Couch. Pursuant to this contract, Couch issued to Bryce 30 checks in the aggregate amount of $35,000. Of these, Bryce endorsed and deposited four checks in the aggregate amount of $9,000 into his own account. At Bryce's direction, Couch delivered the remaining 26 checks in the aggregate amount of $26,000 to Josephine. Josephine endorsed Bryce's name on these checks and deposited them into her own account. Bryce authorized Josephine to use the money "to take care of both of us."

By this action, Bryce seeks to recover the $26,000 received by Josephine. There can be no doubt that Josephine held this money for Bryce. By her contract with him, she had relinquished any right to any of it. He was entitled to recover all of it—unless Columbia Family Code section 6703 stood in the way. Under that provision, a minor under the care of a parent who is unable to provide for him may contract to pay the reasonable value of things necessary for his support and that of his family and may not disaffirm such a contract. This being true, it must follow that the minor can authorize the use of money held for him for those purposes, and cannot recover the money thus paid out.

In entering judgment for Josephine, the trial court found that she expended the $26,000 she had received for herself and for Bryce. That finding, however, was insufficient to support the judgment. The court did not find that Josephine expended the money for herself and for Bryce *for things necessary for their support*. Nor could the court have so found. The evidence showed that, at all relevant times, Josephine had an independent and substantial source of income. It also showed that she expended the $26,000 she had received, as she herself admitted, for the "good things of life," not necessities.

The judgment is reversed.

Brady v. Thomas

Columbia Court of Appeal (2004)

Martha Thomas and her minor son Craig Thomas appeal the judgment in favor of Craig's former personal manager, Sharyn Brady, for unpaid commissions under a contract. Because Craig had a right as a minor to disaffirm the contract, we reverse.

In 1999, Brady entered into an "Artist's Manager's Contract" with Martha and Craig, who was then 10 years old. Martha signed the contract and wrote Craig's name on the signature page where he was designated "Artist." Craig did not sign the contract. Pursuant to the contract, Brady was to act as Craig's exclusive personal manager in exchange for a commission of 15 percent of all consideration paid to Craig as an artist during the three-year term of the contract.

In 2001, Craig obtained a recurring acting role on the Acme Television Network show *The Go-Kart Kid*. Some weeks later, Martha sent a certified letter to Brady stating that Craig no longer needed her management services, could no longer afford to pay her a 15 percent commission because they owed a "huge amount" of taxes, and were thereby "terminating" the contract. Within days, Brady responded, informing Craig that he was in breach.

In 2002, Brady filed suit against Craig for breach of contract. After a bench trial, the court found that Brady had proven her case by a preponderance of the evidence, and awarded her commissions of $154,700. In doing so, it rejected Craig's defense that the contract was invalid because Craig was a minor at the time he entered into it. Craig appealed from the ensuing judgment.

As a general proposition, parental consent is required for the provision of services to minors for the simple reason that minors may disaffirm their own contracts to acquire such services. According to Columbia Family Code section 6701, "[a] minor may make a contract in the same manner as an adult, subject to the power of disaffirmance" provided by Columbia Family Code section 6702. In turn, Columbia Family Code section 6702 states that, generally, "a contract of a minor may be disaffirmed by the minor or by the minor's parent or guardian before majority or within a reasonable time afterwards." The law shields minors from their lack of judgment and experience and under certain conditions vests in them the right to disaffirm their contracts. Although in many instances such disaffirmance may work a hardship upon those who deal with a minor, the right to avoid contracts is conferred by law upon a minor for his protection against his own improvidence and the designs of others. It is the policy of the law to protect a minor against himself and his indiscretions and immaturity as well as against the machinations of other people and to discourage adults from contracting with a minor. Any loss occasioned by the disaffirmance of a minor's contract might have been avoided by declining to enter into the contract in the first place. Simply stated, one who provides a minor with services does so at his or her own risk.

No specific language is required to communicate an intent to disaffirm a minor's contract. A minor's contract may be avoided by any act or word disclosing an unequivocal intent to repudiate its binding force and effect. We find that Martha's certified letter was sufficient to constitute a disaffirmance of the contract by Craig because it stated that Martha and Craig were "terminating" the contract.

Therefore, we conclude that Craig had the right to, and did, disaffirm the contract. Accordingly, the judgment is reversed.

Laredo v. Purcell Fruit Co.

Columbia Supreme Court (1950)

Linda Laredo brought an action for breach of contract against Purcell Fruit Co. In her complaint, Laredo alleged that she had entered into a contract with Purcell, represented by its agent Henry Hand, to sell a crop of oranges for $30,000. In its answer, Purcell denied that it had entered into any such contract of sale, alleging that it had authorized Hand only to enter into a contract of consignment under which it agreed to pack, ship, market, and sell the crop and pay her the net proceeds, which amounted to $10,000. After trial, a jury found in favor of Laredo and awarded her $30,000. Purcell appealed from the ensuing judgment.

Purcell's theory, at trial and on appeal, is that Hand did not have actual authority to make any contract of sale with Laredo. Under Columbia law, actual authority exists "when, at the time of taking action that has legal consequences for the principal, the agent reasonably believes, in accordance with the principal's manifestations to the agent, that the principal wishes the agent so to act." Columbia Civil Code section 3801. Purcell claims that the evidence introduced at trial shows that, at the time of his dealings with Laredo, Hand did not, and could not, reasonably believe that it wished him to enter into any contract of sale.

In contrast, Laredo's theory, at trial and on appeal, is that, at the very least, Hand had the apparent authority to make the contract of sale with her. Under Columbia law, apparent authority exists "when a third party reasonably believes the actor has authority to act on behalf of the principal and that belief is traceable to the principal's manifestations." Columbia Civil Code section 3802. Laredo claims that whatever the evidence introduced at trial might show about Hand's actual authority to enter into the contract of sale with her, it shows his apparent authority to do so.

Laredo's theory prevailed below. It prevails here as well. The evidence introduced at trial establishes the following facts: Over many years, Purcell has entered into contracts of sale as well as contracts of consignment for oranges in Columbia; Hand was Purcell's sole agent in Laredo's area; Hand drove a truck provided to him by Purcell, on which was printed in large, bold letters, "Henry Hand, Agent for Purcell Fruit Co."; Hand had in his possession form contracts of sale printed by Purcell and bearing Purcell's name; Purcell had always performed every contract of sale Hand had entered into, and had never disavowed any; all of these facts were well known to Laredo and to the other orange growers in the area; in addition, Don Gordon, the owner of Purcell, visited Laredo and the other orange growers in the area at the beginning of the season to tell them that Hand would be calling on them. Perhaps Purcell had not granted Hand actual authority to enter into a contract of sale with Laredo on Purcell's behalf. Or perhaps it had revoked such authority before the fact. But that matters not. Hand had apparent authority to enter into a contract of sale with Laredo on Purcell's behalf. Laredo reasonably believed that Hand had authority to act on Purcell's behalf and that belief was traceable to Purcell's own words and conduct. In light of Hand's apparent authority, there was unquestionably a contract of sale between Laredo and Purcell.

The judgment is affirmed.

Performance Test Oct 2020 (Contracts Minority, Necessaries, & Agency)

II. Concise Outline for the Performance Test, October 2020

A. Issue 1: Is Ryan Able to Disaffirm the Contract?

Governing Rule (CF C. § 6702): A contract of a minor may be disaffirmed by the minor or the minor's parent or guardian before majority or within a reasonable time afterwards, unless the contract falls under the necessity exception (§ 6703).

Sub-Issue: Applicability of the "Necessity" Exception (CF C. § 6703)

> **Rule**: The contract cannot be disaffirmed if: (a) it is to pay the reasonable value of things necessary for the support of the minor or family; (b) these things were actually furnished; AND (c) the minor was not under the care of a parent/guardian able to provide.
>
> **Argument for Disaffirmation (Focus on Element C)**: The contract is disaffirmable because the parent (Janice Wright) was able to provide for the minor.
>
> > **Miller v. Miller Controlling Precedent**: The exception does not apply if the parent has an "independent and substantial source of income." The PT fact pattern does not explicitly state Janice's income, but the lack of facts to the contrary suggests she is "able to provide."
>
> **Argument for Disaffirmation (Focus on Element A)**: The "options" (extra weapons, extra lives) are for "enhancement" of a video game experience and are not "necessities" for support, as defined under CF C. § 6703.
>
> > **Miller v. Miller Controlling Precedent**: Spending money on "good things of life" is not spending money on necessities for support. Video game options are definitively not necessities.
>
> **Conclusion**: Ryan is able to disaffirm the contract because the contract does not meet the "necessity" exception: the items were not necessaries and the facts do not support that Janice was unable to provide.

B. Issue 2: Did Janice's Letter Disaffirm the Contract for Ryan?

Governing Rule (CF C. § 6702 / Brady v. Thomas): A parent can disaffirm for the minor. No specific language is required. A contract may be avoided by any act or word disclosing an unequivocal intent to repudiate its binding force and effect (i.e., "terminating" the contract).

Argument for Disaffirmation (YES): Janice's letter (Fact File) demonstrated an unequivocal intent to repudiate the majority of the contract.

She requested a "**reversal of the amount of $8,980 for unauthorized charges**."

This act specifically repudiated the $8,980 portion of the charges, which is the entirety of the over-limit spending.

This action is similar to the mother in **Brady v. Thomas who simply wrote a certified letter stating they were "terminating" the contract** due to tax issues, which the court found sufficient for disaffirmance.

Argument Against Disaffirmation (Counter-Argument/Refutation): GamerTrax might argue the letter was only a request for a reversal of unauthorized charges, not a clear intent to repudiate the contract based on Ryan's minority.

Refutation: The Brady court requires "**any act or word disclosing an unequivocal intent to repudiate**." Requesting a reversal of a specific, large charge based on an authorization limit acts as an unequivocal disaffirmance of that excess amount, satisfying the low bar set by the law.

Conclusion: Janice's letter constitutes a valid disaffirmation of the $8,980 charge on Ryan's behalf.

C. Issue 3: Is Janice Liable for the $8,980 Charge?

Governing Rule (CC C. § 3810): Any act of an agent within the scope of his or her actual or apparent authority binds the principal.

1. Actual Authority (CC C. § 3801, 3803)

Rule: Actual authority exists when the agent (Ryan) reasonably believes the principal (Janice) wishes them to act, based on the principal's manifestations to the agent.

Analysis: Janice gave Ryan explicit permission to open the account and provided the credit card details, but she manifested a clear limit to Ryan: "no more than $20."

Conclusion: Ryan acted outside the scope of his actual authority for the $8,980 excess amount. Janice is NOT bound by actual authority.

2. Apparent Authority (CC C. § 3802, 3804)

Rule: Apparent authority exists when a third party (GamerTrax) reasonably believes the actor (Ryan) has authority to act on behalf of the principal (Janice), and that belief is traceable to the principal's manifestations (CC C. § 3802).

Argument Against Liability (Focus on Principal's Manifestations): Janice's only manifestation to GamerTrax was verifying that Ryan had permission to open the account. GamerTrax's Terms of Service required the minor's parent to verify they gave permission.

> The only manifestation from Janice to the third party was permission to open the account, not to spend any amount.
>
> Ryan's Terms of Service (TOS) stated, "I further agree that I am authorized to use the valid credit or debit card provided in any and all amounts, up to and including the limit established by the issuer." **Janice did not agree to this TOS; Ryan did**.
>
> **Laredo v. Purcell Fruit Co. Controlling Precedent**: Apparent authority requires the third party's belief to be traceable to the principal's own words and conduct. Janice's only conduct was verifying the opening of the account and giving the card details to her son. Her private limit of $20 is irrelevant, but the fact that her manifestation to GamerTrax was limited to permission is key.

Conclusion: Janice is NOT liable for the $8,980 charge on the basis of apparent authority, as her manifestation to GamerTrax did not establish authority for unlimited use, and Ryan's subsequent agreement to the TOS cannot bind her.

Performance Test Oct 2020 (Contracts Minority, Necessaries, & Agency)

III. Comprehensive Guide for the Performance Test, October 2020

Initial Read Through

Audience & Format: The audience is your supervising attorney, Margery Turner. The format is an Objective Memorandum. Critically, the task memo explicitly states: "Do not include a statement of facts in your memorandum."

Assignment: The memo must answer three separate, specific legal questions in a neutral, objective tone.

Required Sections: The final document must include a Question Presented (or Issue), Brief Answer (or Conclusion), and a detailed Discussion section for each of the three questions.

Next, quickly review the File and Library to understand the content. Note the statutes address Minority (Family Code) and Agency (Civil Code), and the cases provide context for "necessity," "disaffirmance method," and "apparent authority."

Precise Issue Spotting

The Task Memo explicitly provides the three main issues. Your goal is to translate these questions into IRAC-ready legal Issues that guide your analysis:

1. Is Ryan able to disaffirm the contract? → Issue 1: Whether Ryan, as a minor, is able to disaffirm the contract with GamerTrax given the exception for necessaries.

2. If so, did Janice's letter disaffirm the contract for Ryan? → Issue 2: Whether Janice's letter to GamerTrax constitutes a legally sufficient disaffirmation of the contract on Ryan's behalf.

3. Is Janice liable for the $8,980 charge? → Issue 3: Whether Janice Wright is liable for the $8,980 charge based on theories of actual or apparent agency authority.

Key Facts

Issue 1 (Disaffirmance) Facts:

Ryan is 12 years old (minor).

Purchases are for "extra weapons" and "extra lives" (game "options" / "enhancements").

Janice is his parent/guardian and there is no evidence she is unable to provide.

Issue 2 (Disaffirmation Method) Facts:

Janice sent a letter requesting a "**reversal of the amount of $8,980 for unauthorized charges**."

GamerTrax declined the request.

Issue 3 (Agency Liability) Facts:

Janice gave Ryan permission to open the account and provided her card details.

She manifested **a clear private limit of $20** to Ryan.

Ryan clicked "I agree" to TOS stating he was authorized "in any and all amounts".

Janice verified permission to open the account with GamerTrax.

Structuring the Answer

CAPTION/HEADER: Include TO:, FROM:, DATE:, and RE: (e.g., RE: Potential Wright Litigation).

QUESTIONS PRESENTED: Rephrase the three Task Memo questions into neutral, formal legal issues.

BRIEF ANSWERS: Provide a short, direct answer (a single sentence or two) for each of the three questions.

DISCUSSION: This section houses the full IRAC analysis for each of the three issues. Use clear subheadings corresponding to the Questions Presented (e.g., I. Ryan is able to disaffirm the contract...).

Step by Step Process

Step 1: Analyze Minor's Disaffirmance (Issue 1)

Rule: Start with the general rule that a minor may disaffirm (§ 6702). Immediately pivot to the only defense available to GamerTrax: the Necessities Exception (§ 6703).

Application Strategy: Argue against the exception by attacking its elements.

Attack (a) "Necessaries": Argue that video game "options" are not things "necessary for the support." Use Miller v. Miller to analogize that these are "good things of life," not necessities.

Attack (c) Parent's Ability to Provide: Absent evidence that Janice is impoverished, the legal presumption favors the parent's ability to provide, reinforcing the minor's right to disaffirm.

Conclusion: Ryan can disaffirm the contract because the items are not necessities.

Step 2: Analyze Disaffirmance Method (Issue 2)

Rule: The rule is simple and highly favorable to the client: A parent can disaffirm for the minor, and Brady v. Thomas clarifies that no specific language is required—only an "unequivocal intent to repudiate."

Application Strategy: Argue that Janice's letter requesting a reversal of the $8,980 unauthorized charge shows an unequivocal intent to repudiate that portion of the contract, satisfying the low bar set by Brady.

Conclusion: Janice's letter constitutes a valid disaffirmation.

Step 3: Analyze Janice's Liability/Agency (Issue 3)

Rule: The principal (Janice) is bound only by an agent's (Ryan's) acts within the scope of Actual or Apparent Authority (§ 3810).

Sub-Analysis A: Actual Authority:

> **Rule**: Authority exists based on the principal's manifestation to the agent (§ 3801).
>
> **Application**: Janice's manifestation to Ryan included a specific limit ($20). Ryan spent $8,980. **Conclusion: No actual authority for the excess**.

Sub-Analysis B: Apparent Authority:

> **Rule**: Authority exists when a third party (GamerTrax) reasonably believes the agent has authority, and that belief is traceable to the principal's manifestations to the third party (§ 3802, § 3804).
>
> **Application Strategy (Crux of the Issue)**: Janice's only manifestation to GamerTrax was verifying permission to open the account. GamerTrax's belief that Ryan had unlimited authority is based on Ryan's agreement to the TOS ("authorized... in any and all amounts"), not Janice's manifestations. Use Laredo v. Purcell Fruit Co. to argue that GamerTrax cannot trace its belief in unlimited authority back to Janice's words or conduct. **Conclusion: Janice is NOT liable based on apparent authority**.

Overall Conclusion: Janice is not liable based on either actual or apparent authority.

Performance Test Oct 2020 (Contracts Minority, Necessaries, & Agency)

IV. Ultra Concise Answer, Performance Test, October 2020

TO: Margery Turner
FROM: Applicant
DATE: October 6, 2020
RE: Potential Wright Litigation

QUESTIONS PRESENTED

Whether Ryan, a minor, may disaffirm the contract with GamerTrax given that the purchases were not for necessities.

Whether Janice Wright's letter to GamerTrax constitutes a legally sufficient disaffirmation of the contract on Ryan's behalf.

Whether Janice Wright is liable for the unauthorized $8,980 charge based on actual or apparent agency authority.

BRIEF ANSWERS

Yes. Ryan may disaffirm the contract because the game "options" are not things necessary for his support, and the necessaries exception to disaffirmance does not apply.

Yes. Janice's letter constitutes a valid disaffirmation because the law requires no specific language, only an unequivocal intent to repudiate the unauthorized charges.

No. Janice is not liable because Ryan acted without actual authority, and GamerTrax cannot reasonably trace any belief in unlimited authority back to Janice's limited manifestations.

DISCUSSION

I. Ryan is able to disaffirm the contract.

A minor may generally disaffirm a contract before majority or within a reasonable time afterward (Fam. Code § 6702). GamerTrax's only potential defense is the Necessities Exception (Fam. Code § 6703). The exception fails because the "extra weapons" and "extra lives" are enhancements, not items necessary for support; Miller v. Miller limits the exception to necessities, not the "good things of life." Furthermore, Janice is his parent and able to provide. Ryan may therefore disaffirm the contract.

II. Janice's letter constitutes a legally sufficient disaffirmation.

A contract of a minor may be disaffirmed by the minor's parent (Fam. Code § 6702). No specific language is required, only an unequivocal intent to repudiate (Brady v. Thomas). Janice's letter explicitly requested a "reversal of the amount of $8,980 for unauthorized charges." This clearly communicates her intent to repudiate the contract's unauthorized portion.

III. Janice is not liable for the $8,980 charge.

A principal is bound only by an agent's acts within the scope of actual or apparent authority (Civ. Code § 3810). Ryan lacked Actual Authority because Janice manifested a clear private limit of $20 to him (Civ. Code § 3801). He also lacked Apparent Authority because GamerTrax's belief in his authority (based on his assent to the TOS) is traceable to Ryan's actions, not Janice's manifestations to them (Civ. Code § 3802). Janice's only manifestation to GamerTrax was verifying permission to open the account, which is insufficient to bind her to unlimited charges (Laredo v. Purcell Fruit Co.).

Author Bio:

Ray Hayden, JD.

Ray developed this methodology after concluding that success on the California General Bar Exam (CGBX) is not about knowing every rule, but about **the execution process** under time constraints. Through his focused study and analytical breakdown of the exam, he identified a gap in existing prep materials: they teach law, but fail to provide a precise, repeatable strategy for creating a passing answer.

Hayden's work led to the **CGBX: A Three Step System**, a proprietary system built for analytical precision. His methodology (featuring the Concise Outline, the detailed Comprehensive Guide, and Ultra Concise Answer) is engineered to translate complex legal analysis into defensible, solid scoring exam answers.

Ray is personally dedicated to helping every law student optimize their performance. His passion is creating efficient, high yield solutions that reduce complexity and deliver maximum results, ensuring you're equipped not just with knowledge, but an optimized strategic process to produce defensible answers that demonstrate the required standard of competence.

SUPPLEMENTAL MATERIALS

PERFORMANCE TEST INSTRUCTIONS

1. This performance test is designed to evaluate your ability to handle a select number of legal authorities in the context of a factual problem.

2. The problem is set in the fictional State of Columbia, one of the United States. In Columbia, the intermediate appellate court is the Court of Appeal and the highest court is the Supreme Court.

3. You will have two sets of materials with which to work: a File and a Library.

4. The File consists of source documents containing all the facts of the case. The first document in the File is a memorandum containing the directions for the task you are to complete. The other documents in the File contain information about your case and may include some facts that are not relevant. Facts are sometimes ambiguous, incomplete, or even conflicting. As in practice, a client's or supervising attorney's version of events may be incomplete or unreliable. Applicants are expected to recognize when facts are inconsistent or missing and are expected to identify sources of additional facts.

5. The Library contains the legal authorities needed to complete the task and may also include some authorities that are not relevant to the assigned lawyering task. The cases, statutes, regulations, or rules may be real, modified, or written solely for the purpose of this performance test. If any of them appear familiar to you, do not assume that they are precisely the same as you have read before. Read each thoroughly, as if it were new to you. You should assume that cases were decided in the jurisdictions and on the dates shown. In citing cases from the Library, you may use abbreviations and omit page references. Applicants are expected to extract from the Library the legal principles necessary to analyze the problem and perform the task.

6. In answering this performance test, you should concentrate on the materials in the File and Library. What you have learned in law school and elsewhere provides the general background for analyzing the problem; the File and Library provide the specific materials with which you must work.

7. This performance test is designed to be completed in 90 minutes. Although there are no restrictions or parameters on how you apportion that 90 minutes, you should allow yourself sufficient time to thoroughly review the materials and organize your planned response before you begin writing it. Since the time allotted for this session of the examination includes two (2) essay questions in addition to this performance test, time management is essential.

PERFORMANCE TEST INSTRUCTIONS **(Continued on Next Page)**

<u>PERFORMANCE TEST INSTRUCTIONS</u> (Continued)

8. Do not include your actual name or any other identifying information anywhere in the work product required by the task memorandum.

9. Your performance test answer will be graded on its responsiveness to and compliance with directions regarding the task you are to complete, as well as on its content, thoroughness, and organization.

THE THREE STEP SYSTEM:

Every essay and performance test in each series is broken down into a Three Step System, designed to move you from analysis to execution with precision.

The Three Step System: Your Integrated Advantage

Each guide is engineered to help you internalize the required material and clearly demonstrate competence beyond the minimum required for the California General Bar Exam.

1. **Concise Outline**: The crucial first step. The outline distills the fact pattern to the essential issues required for a solid answer, and confirms your issue spotting, and organizational strategy.

2. **Comprehensive Guide**: This is your strategic workshop, a demonstration on how to construct a defensible answer that achieves the required standard of competence from start to finish.

3. **Ultra Concise Answer**: This is the tightest answer you can realistically write on exam day, structured to aid in demonstrating the required competence.

Practice your execution, trust the integrated process, and write with unwavering confidence.

Now, Go Execute.

VDO1